A University Education for the 21st Century:
The Opening of the American Mind

Fr. Juan R. Vélez

Foreword by Most Reverend James D. Conley

The legend on the seal of Oxford University reads *Dominus Illuminatio Mea,* the opening words of psalm 27, a reminder that knowledge comes from God who enlightens man's reason.

ISBN-13: 978-1507862698 (CreateSpace-Assigned)
ISBN-10: 1507862695

Cover design: Mariana Roo
Cover Image: All Souls College, University of Oxford
Looking through the gateway into the North Quadrangle and the imposing Gothic towers designed by Nicholas Hawksmoor.
Photo by David Stowell (Creative Commons Attribution-ShareAlike)

TABLE OF CONTENTS

DEDICATION 6

ACKNOWLEDGMENTS..7

ENDORSEMENTS...8

FOREWORD 11

    by Most Reverend James D. Conley................11

PREFACE 15

INTRODUCTION 17

I. THE PURPOSE OF A UNIVERSITY EDUCATION...............25

    Learning for Learning's Sake................................30

    Other Ends of the University 33

II. A CRISIS OF LIBERAL ARTS EDUCATION 38

    Two Models of Core Curriculum.............................39

    Study of a Top Liberal Arts College........................42

    A Classical Core Curriculum.................................46

III. CHOOSING THE RIGHT COLLEGE.............................52

    Personal Objectives 54

    Selection Criteria 55

    Finances..58

    Other Considerations...60

    Deliberation and Decision Making........................61

VI. GOD IN THE UNIVERSITY CLASSROOMS...................63

    Anti-Catholic Prejudice 66

    Why Students Should Study About God....................69

    What is Natural Theology? 70

    What do we Know About God? 73

    Bringing God Back to the Classrooms....................77

V. THE CLASSICS AND WESTERN CULTURE 80

The Influence of Classical Greek Literature 82

Roman Literature and Culture...85

Latin and Transmission of Western Culture.........................88

VI. STUDY & PRACTICE OF SCIENCES AT THE UNIVERSITY AND BEYOND ...96

Natural Sciences & Applied Sciences in the Modern University 97

History of Natural Sciences...98

Foundations and Limits of Science.....................................101

Harmony Between Science and Faith 103

Liberal Arts Courses for Science Majors.............................107

VII. ADVERSITIES FACED AND CONTRIBUTIONS MADE BY CATHOLICS IN UNIVERSITY LIFE 110

The Spiritual Life of Christian Students 111

Catholic Student Centers on Campus 116

A Community of Friends 120

VIII. WHAT FOLLOWS COLLEGE AND A LIBERAL ARTS DEGREE? 126

Graduate Studies..128

Professional Schools...131

Future Generations 137

CONCLUSION...142

APPENDIX A: Questions to Ask Before Applying to a College or University...147

APPENDIX B: First Medieval Universities and their Origins...........149

Irish Monasteries...151

English Monasteries 153

Charlemagne's Schools...154

Bologna and the First Universities......................................156

Colleges and Halls..159

Universities and Seminaries: L'École des Hautes Études.........161

BIBLIOGRAPHY 164

4

INDEX...169

ABOUT THE AUTHOR 176

DEDICATION

Amicis meis

Bruce, Barbara, Katherine Wyman,

James et Susan Ridlen atque Pat Sharp,

hunc libellum

propter operem fidemque eorum

per multos annos datum dedico.

ACKNOWLEDGMENTS

This book has been written with the insights and advice of friends, both students and professors. Over the last sixteen years - many of these as chaplain at various university centers run by Opus Dei - I have shared the joys and sorrows of students, their ambitions and difficulties. They have taught me a great deal.

I wish to thank the many people who have directly assisted me with material or suggestions for this manuscript. Bruce and Barbara Wyman, Robert Constable, Steve Justice, Ignacio Rodriguez, Anthony Adamthwaite, Santiago Schnell, John Hulsman, Cornelia Tsakiridou, Christopher Tollefsen, Thomas A. Cavanaugh, Kathleen Schmainda, and Gonzalo Herranz read the entire manuscript or large parts of it and offered me valuable criticism and suggestions. Although due to the nature of this work I was only able to respond to some of their observations I am very grateful to them. Naturally, the opinions expressed here are my own. The Most Reverend James D. Conley, Bishop of Lincoln, graciously wrote the Foreword.

Susan Ridlen, Patricia Sharp and Mariana Roo provided me with very generous editorial assistance as well as Salvina Ulfindo who prepared the index. Many others, such as Peter Dowbor, Francisco Ruiz, Maria Marsella, Allison Coates, Alvaro José Cifuentes and the men at Darien Study Center have given me their encouragement and advice. I am also grateful to them.

Lastly, I wish to express gratitude to my parents, Rodrigo and Maria Vélez, who always instilled in my siblings and me a desire for learning and an appreciation for history, art and music through visits to historical sites and museums as well as attendance at musical performances.

ENDORSEMENTS

"Juan Vélez writes for students who are forming their mind and will, seeking a liberal arts education within the current context of great American universities and colleges. Vélez writes in the tradition of James Schall, Allan Bloom, Mark Henrie and, preeminently, his spiritual mentor, John Henry Newman. The book is a readable guide for the student who will ultimately need to create his own curriculum in the Western tradition, following some aspects of the traditional seven liberal arts."
Robert T. Constable DSW
Professor Emeritus
Loyola University Chicago

"A University Education for the 21st Century is a wonderfully sane and invaluable guide for parents and students on the value of a liberal arts education and how to access it in an increasingly secular and scientific academy. Father Juan Vélez's experience with students as a chaplain in American universities deepens and enriches a beautifully clear, concise and compelling text."
Anthony Adamthwaite
Professor, Department of History
University of California at Berkeley

In my view, A University Education for the 21st Century is a persuasive invitation to students to enrich their intellectual life by paying attention to the humanities, learning each day from the intellectual giants of mankind. In words of Sir William Osler, these students should strive "to get the education if not of a scholar, at least of a gentleman."
Gonzalo Herranz
Professor Emeritus, Pathology and Medical Ethics
University of Navarre

"A compelling and spirited defense of a liberal arts education, <u>A University Education for the 21st Century</u> by Father Juan Vélez beautifully transmits the values at the core of academia. This book will enrich the thinking of humanists and scientists alike".
Ignacio Rodriguez-Iturbe
James S. McDonnell Distinguished University Professor and
Professor of Civil and Environmental Engineering
Princeton University

Juan Vélez's little book should be of interest to anyone concerned about the state of higher education, but it is particularly useful as a vade mecum for the serious high school graduate who is about to make the exciting but perilous choice of a college. This in an era that is unsure even of the purpose of a higher education and the liberal arts tradition that remains precariously its core. Guided by the spirit of John Henry Newman, Father Juan combines a history of liberal education and the university with a lively critique of its contemporary failings, whether the politicization of the classroom, tireless debunking of the West, contempt for idealism, or abject careerism. There follows a strong argument for fundamental reform as well as abundant practical advice for choosing colleges and courses that cultivate true learning. There has never been a greater need for academic (and spiritual) mentoring, and this book serves that purpose well.
John Hulsman
Emeritus Professor of English
Rider College

<u>*A University Education for the 21st Century*</u> *answers questions that should be on the minds of all reflective young people: why study the liberal arts? Where would it be best for me to do so? And how, once in college or university, should I go about seeking an education that will shape both my intellect and will? Many high schools and universities do not provide sound guidance for young men and women asking these questions; Fr. Vélez's book will be welcome and essential reading for them.*
Christopher Tollefsen
Professor of Philosophy
University of South Carolina

After reading A University Education for the 21st Century even those seeking an education in science and engineering will be convinced of the need for a liberal arts curriculum. Now more than ever, it is critical that those on the front lines of discovery and innovation with great potential for lasting and widespread impact seek an authentic humanistic formation. Fr Juan Vélez's experience as a physician, priest and university chaplain makes him especially suited to provide both the philosophical motivation as well as practical advice for achieving this formation. This book will inspire students and their parents.
Katheen M. Schmainda PhD
Professor, Radiology & Biophysics
Medical College of Wisconsin

Fr. Juan Vélez's A University Education for the 21st Century, presents a concise and substantive argument for the perennial value of a liberal arts education and its importance to Catholic higher education. It is essential reading for Catholic educators and for prospective college students and their parents who value the rich tradition of the Church.
Cornelia A. Tsakiridou, Ph.D.
Associate Professor, Philosophy
Director, Diplomat-In-Residence Program
La Salle University, Philadelphia

Father Velez's book, A University Education for the 21st Century: The Opening of the American Mind, is an excellent resource and provides a wonderful reflection for parents, students and high school counselors who are navigating the complex world of college selection and admissions. This book will be a valuable reference for many years to come.
Msgr. Sal Pilato
Superintendent of High Schools, Archdiocese of Los Angeles

10

by Most Reverend James D. Conley

I came to the Catholic faith in the 1970s, during my undergraduate years at a public university in Kansas. On its face, that setting seems among the most unlikely places in which to encounter Jesus Christ and his Church. But, the Pearson Integrated Humanities Program specialized in the unlikely, and the extraordinary.

From approximately 1970 to 1980, three professors at the University of Kansas drew students into the riches of the Western intellectual tradition—forming their minds, their imaginations and their hearts, for friendship, and humility, and wonder. In less than a decade, a public university in Kansas formed two future bishops, an abbot, monks, priests and religious, and hundreds of men and women who've been reborn in wonder, and reborn in Jesus Christ.

At the very heart of the Integrated Humanities Program was the work of my spiritual patron, the great British convert Blessed John Henry Cardinal Newman. A prolific author he wrote eloquently on theology, history and literature. He brought a unique religious community to England, and oversaw its expansion. He preached beautifully and his sermons have become classics. But the great apostolic project of his Catholic life was the formation and education of Catholics who would know and love the faith, which would be the basis from which they undertook every other kind of noble project in their lives.

Newman founded the Catholic University of Ireland, and also the first English boarding school for Catholic gentlemen since the Tudor Reformation. And in his intellectual work, most especially *The Idea of a University*, Newman outlined the principles by which any university, Catholic or otherwise, should undertake its solemn mission.

A university, said Newman, is "a place of *teaching* universal *knowledge*". A university trains the intellect to reason, so that students will possess the "faculty of entering with comparative ease into any subject of thought, and of taking up with aptitude any

11

science or profession." Newman reasoned that to succeed, a university had to undertake its work with a commitment to "educate the intellect to reason well in all matters, to reach out towards truth, and to grasp it."

In short, Newman wrote that every university should be a place where young minds are able seek out and discern what is true, what is good, and what is beautiful.

Today, education in many places has been overcome by our cultural tendencies towards technocratic reasoning and a utilitarian preoccupation with earnings. Technical possibility has become the common standard of moral responsibility. The minute specialization of scientific and technological research in modern universities discourages reasoned reflection on the relationship between scientific advancement and moral goods. And the role of history, literature, poetry and philosophy is ever diminished—the humanities regarded too often as a curiosity; a tolerable deviation from the real work of career preparation. Too often, modern universities train students for earning and producing, without really preparing them for living.

In *The Idea of a University,* Newman wrote that "men whose minds are possessed with some one object, take exaggerated views of its importance, are feverish in the pursuit of it, make it the measure of things which are utterly foreign to it, and are startled and despond if it happens to fail them.... But the intellect, which has been disciplined to the perfection of its powers, which knows, and thinks while it knows, which has learned to leaven the dense mass of facts and events with the elastic force of reason, such an intellect cannot be partial, cannot be exclusive, cannot be impetuous, cannot be at a loss, cannot but be patient, collected, and majestically calm, because it discerns the end in every beginning, the origin in every end, the law in every interruption, the limit in each delay; because it ever knows where it stands, and how its path lies from one point to another."

The antidote to the problem of modern universities is the formation of minds that think with the "elastic force of reason." This requires a revival of the classical approach to university formation—a revival of the poetic imagination, of formation in history and philosophy. Minds that know how to reason are the products of hearts and imaginations that have been transformed by wonder.

On secular campuses and Catholic universities, educators must become as intentional about human and spiritual formation as they are about the transmission of scientific and technical knowledge.

In *A University Education*, Fr. Juan Vélez provides practical reflections on the history and mission of universities. He offers insights for students and parents on the process of finding a truly meaningful university education, and he offers sober reflections for university administrators about the needs of modern students and the formation of meaningful university curricula.

There are many Catholic colleges and universities across the country committed to forming minds to know the truth, and hearts to choose the good. And there are excellent Newman Centers and Catholic Studies Institutes at dozens of secular universities, offering intellectual and personal formation to students seeking to know and serve Jesus Christ. *A University Education* is a useful guide for parents and students discerning the place in which God might be calling them to study.

A University Education is important for anyone concerned with the state of higher education in the United States, and the consequences for the Church, for souls, and for the world. It presents critical insights about the relationship between education, formation, and Christian discipleship. Newman wrote that "religious truth is not only a portion, but a condition of general knowledge. To blot it out is nothing short, if I may so speak, of unraveling the web of University Teaching." *A University Education* offers historical and practical wisdom about the integration of Jesus Christ, and his Church, into the university formation of disciples, ready to reason, work, and live in the light of Truth.

There are two questions of prime importance to every student considering college. To understand the questions sufficiently is to understand how to ensure a successful college or university experience. To misunderstand the questions is to misunderstand what is at stake in this decision, a misunderstanding that could jeopardize the soul. The first question is, "What is a good college education?" This question seems very straightforward, but in reality, it is quite complex. The second question is, "How do I get this kind of education?" This text attempts to offer answers to both questions, drawing primarily from John Henry Newman, a lifelong educator, and other great thinkers.

These answers will make this great adventure comprehensible and rewarding. Throughout this text, the reader will be reminded that truth, beauty, goodness and everlasting happiness are at stake on every college campus.

A university is an institution of higher education that, in addition to undergraduate courses and degrees, offers graduate courses and degrees. The term "college" was initially given to a group of students and teachers within a university who lived and studied in the same buildings. By extension, the term came to refer to an individual school within a university, for example, a college of nursing or engineering. In the United States, the name "college" has been applied to an institution of higher learning, usually smaller than a university, where the emphasis is on teaching rather than research, and doctoral degrees are not conferred. In this book, however, the terms university and college will be used interchangeably.

This book does not pretend to be an original work. Other authors, most notably Allan Bloom, have examined with detail and accuracy the crisis of higher education in America in the second half of the 20th century. It aspires to continue this important discussion and assist students who are looking for a good education, resisting the temptation to succumb to the selfish materialism and intellectual relativism of our age.

For readers in high school, it offers a vision of a liberal arts education that they can already begin to acquire while in high school. For those who are already undergraduates in liberal arts or in science-oriented careers, this is a stimulus to think more about how they are approaching and benefiting from their college education. And for those who have graduated from college, recently or many years ago, it can serve as a reminder that intellectual and cultural formation is a lifetime endeavor that engages us in reading the Classics, discussions with friends, visits to museums and attendance at musical performances.

Although most students can benefit from these considerations, they are especially applicable to those attending four-year colleges and universities. These observations, taken from my work as a chaplain for students from select institutions of higher education on the East and West Coasts of the United States, corroborate the findings and insights of scholars. I also draw from my own experience, once as a medical student and resident in internal medicine and afterwards as a Bachelor of Arts and Doctor in Theology.

As Allen Bloom argues in *The Closing of the American Mind*, the "virtue of openness" to everything except Western Thought and Virtues has closed the mind of youth. Our society has fallen into a devastating cultural relativism and skepticism regarding truth and goodness. Only a return to the spirit of a classical liberal arts education can begin to open the minds of young people in the 21st century. This book is a modest attempt to help young men and women to come out of the shadows of the cave described by Plato and into the light of the day, seeking and finding answers to the fundamental questions about God and about their existence.

A liberal arts education enlarges the mind of men and women and cultivates the powers of their souls.

Darien, Illinois
December 25, 2014

More young adults are attending college than ever before. These young men and women come from a wide variety of backgrounds, with varying levels of preparedness for the college experience. Yet never before has the college experience been so hazardous to the intellectual and moral welfare of the youth. The university, originally founded upon Christian principles, has become, in many instances, hostile to these very principles and everything related to religion. Many students are adrift, not understanding the nature of a true education, namely, the reason for university studies or the potential dangers that face them. Often their parents are equally unaware of just what happens behind the ivy-covered walls of the university. Yet, it is still possible to obtain the right kind of education, one that cultivates the soul and prepares a student not only for a livelihood but also for eternity.

This book invites a student to consider these questions: What is the purpose of a university and a university education? Is there a point to studying liberal arts in our scientific and technological culture?

A typical response a student might give to the first question would be, 'to obtain a degree.' And if asked the purpose of the degree, the student would most likely answer, 'to obtain a better paying job after college,' even though statistics confirm the reality of unemployed or underemployed persons with undergraduate and graduate degrees.[1]

---

[1] Notwithstanding this, between 2000 and 2013, the unemployment rate for individuals without a bachelor's degree was generally higher than the rate for their peers with at least a bachelor's degree. In 2013, for example, the unemployment rate for young adults was 29.2 percent for those who did not complete high school, 17.5 percent for those whose highest level of education was high school completion, and 12.2 percent for those with some college education, compared with an unemployment rate of 7.0 percent for those with at least a bachelor's degree.
"The Condition of Education: Labor force participation and Unemployment Rates by Educational Attainment," U.S. Department of Education and National Center for Education Statistics. Last updated May 2014.

As for the answer to the second question, most consider liberal arts irrelevant for their future work. Many students go to college to prepare for careers in science or to study engineering; others, to prepare for professional schools in law, medicine or business. They do not understand the importance of liberal arts, either as a major or as a part of their undergraduate studies. But the truth is, most students and parents have not really considered either of these questions in any depth. Therein lies the first challenge. Without knowing what they are seeking, they will most likely find something other than a true university education.

There are other challenges, which add to the difficulty of obtaining a true university education. The significant and rising cost of higher education makes students and families think much more about what schools they can afford, and look for scholarships and government loans. In the decades between 2001-2002 and 2011-2012, the cost of undergraduate tuition, room and board rose 40% at public institutions and 28% at private and nonprofit institutions.[2]

The belief that college degrees are necessary to qualify for most higher-paying jobs is certainly a valid reason for obtaining a university education but, as will be argued here, a more important reason for university studies is the development of one's intellectual and moral habits as a person. To learn, to acquire knowledge is the object of the intellect, the highest faculty of our soul. Intellectual growth and learning should be the primary reason to spend four years at college, investing so much money and effort. This period of a person's life is also an important time to mature in character by means of the growth in human and supernatural virtues through the pursuit of a true university education.

---

http://nces.ed.gov/programs/coe/indicator_cbc.asp
[2]This increase was after adjustment for inflation.
"Fast Facts: Tuition costs of colleges and universities," U.S. Department of Education, National Center for Education Statistics (2013) and the Digest of Education Statistics, 2012 (NCES 2014-015), Chapter 3. Accessed November 10, 2014, http://nces.ed.gov/fastfacts/display.asp?id=76

This book will often turn to the writings of John Henry Newman, a great English scholar and priest, author of *The Idea of a University* and *Rise and Progress of Universities*.[3] Newman (1801-1890) was born in London and studied at Oxford University where he also later taught. In 1845, he converted from the Anglican to the Catholic Church. In 1847, he was ordained a Catholic priest and returned to Birmingham, England. He spent the rest of his life there except for a period during 1854-1858 in which he lived in Ireland, founding, at the behest of the Irish bishops, the Catholic University of Ireland in Dublin.

In 1854, the year in which the Catholic University of Ireland opened, Newman delivered a number of lectures on the nature and scope of university education, later published as *The Idea of a University*. Today we live in an age with different social, educational and religious circumstances, yet several of Newman's main ideas present a sound vision of the nature of university education.

One of his major ideas is the notion, to be explored in chapter one, that knowledge is valuable for its own sake. Learning is something good in itself aside from any practical applications derived from such learning. Knowledge often has an instrumental value since it leads to applied science and technology, but even before that, knowledge is its own reward; it is valuable for its own sake.

Newman described a university as a place where wise men, who are teachers, are to be found. He writes: "We must come to the teachers of wisdom to learn wisdom; we must repair to the fountain, and drink there." A university should be a center, a place that brings together the best. "It is the place for great preachers, great orators, great nobles, great statesmen. In the nature of things, greatness and unity go together; excellence implies a centre." A university has

---

[3] *Rise and Progress of Universities* consists of twenty-nine articles Newman wrote for the *Catholic University Gazette*. It first appeared as a volume under the title *University Sketches*, and was later published in *Historical Sketches,* a volume with other essays by Newman. See Paul Shrimpton, *The 'Making of Men,' The Idea and Reality of Newman's university in Oxford and Dublin,* (Leominster: Gracewing, 2014), 118-119.

buildings and traditions; it offers classes and confers degrees, but above all, it is - or should be - a place with excellent teachers and eager students. In other words, an ideal university is a community that pursues truth through the interaction of teachers and students. The highest knowledge is called philosophy, the Greek term for love of wisdom. This philosophy is more than a theory; it is a way of life based on a world vision that pursues the truth.

Unfortunately, the reality of the modern university is far from the university envisioned by Newman or earlier thinkers. The politically correct reality of contemporary universities with their superficial, narrow and disconnected approach to subjects is disconcerting and contrary to the origins of the university: the pursuit of knowledge and the cultivation of the intellect. The extent to which this crisis in higher education affects institutions varies. This sad state of affairs, however, does not invalidate a university education as a whole because the degree to which schools are affected by this university culture varies, as does the individual beliefs of its professors. The choice of a school and the choice of professors and subjects are, nonetheless, very important for a worthwhile university education. As in ancient times, the choice of a teacher should determine the choice of a place for study. Youth went to Athens and much later to Bologna, Oxford or Paris pursuing particular teachers, men like Plato, Aristotle, Roger Bacon, Albert the Great, and Thomas Aquinas.

The crisis of skepticism and relativism faced by universities has a less immediate and visible effect on students of natural sciences and engineering. Instead, it has impoverished the liberal arts and its connection with tradition and wisdom. Furthermore, the growth of biological and other empirical sciences, as well as business sciences with their corresponding career opportunities, turns the question about a university education into a different question: Is a liberal arts education still useful? People rightly wonder: Is such an education meaningful? If the liberal arts provide few answers or answers with little certainty compared to the so-called "hard sciences", it seems pointless to study liberal arts. It is, however, simplistic to conclude that the liberal arts do not lead to knowledge. They certainly do not formulate answers as facts or numbers that can be measured, as in the natural sciences. Instead, they offer answers to questions of a different type: questions about the meaning of things and events.

They explore the ultimate reasons for human and divine actions. They help students to develop a philosophical habit of mind, to understand the whole of society, and the relations of the parts to the whole. It is true that the natural sciences also ask the question 'Why,' but by the nature of their methods and the material objects, the 'Why' of their study refers to material processes.[4]

Beyond the question of the meaningfulness of an education in liberal arts, which will be discussed further in other chapters, students and parents question its practical usefulness. How will such an education prepare me for a job? How will it help me procure employment that can provide for a family? These questions need to be addressed in different ways but, in the first place, it is important to resist a reductive view of man in which employment and earning decides a person's career and way of thinking. There is a false dichotomy between making a living and not pursuing personal educational goals. It is best when persons can do both and not face the 'either or' choice.

Given the confusion produced by relativism and political correctness in higher education, it is very hard to get a proper liberal arts education in today's university. Nonetheless, it is still possible on most college and university campuses. Some schools make it easier, while others nearly impossible. This book will help the student and their parents discern which is which and how to select courses that favor intellectual and spiritual formation.

Often both students and parents must sacrifice in order to afford a university education. Those who do should get the most out of their sacrifice. This is much more than saying, "get the most for your money." Higher education affords students much more than a degree and future monetary return. College years are a unique time for intellectual growth as well as developing good character traits and establishing meaningful lifelong friendships. A significant part of the education consists of the books read and discussed with peers and teachers, the in-depth conversations with friends about the

---

[4] This does not mean that natural scientists do not have interest and sometimes formal training in the philosophical or theological questions that address the question "Why?"

21

important things in life and learning from difficulties and suffering. These years are a time to form deeper convictions about one's religious beliefs and life goals. All of this is the cultivation of the mind and wisdom fostered by the liberal arts tradition.

It is thus a great opportunity to study at a good university or college, and those who have the aptitude and interest to do so are fortunate. However, it is just as important for students to have a clear understanding of the purpose of a university education as well as the contemporary culture of most universities. Within higher education, a liberal arts education remains a possible and enriching choice despite the significant trend towards careers in business, biological and applied sciences. Universities and colleges still offer liberal arts programs, and some of these are quite good. Many others have programs, which regardless of their weaknesses still offer the possibility of obtaining a liberal arts education. Those who graduate with majors in the liberal arts will be enriched by their studies and will be able to apply the knowledge gained to whatever work they may undertake or to the professional schools they may choose to pursue.

In the end, the pursuit of higher education and of a liberal arts education for the sake of learning is a noble goal, something very worthwhile. In the obtainment of this goal, the choice of a school, the choice of a mentor and the choice of at least certain professors make a great difference.

These considerations can challenge students who are enrolled in science majors to take a fresh look at the Humanities and reexamine their assumptions about scientific truth and certainty. They can choose to complete their university education by taking some courses in liberal arts, thus broadening and complementing their perspective on life.

It is also the case, as will be discussed in the chapter on liberal arts, that most schools do not offer good core curriculum for undergraduates. Students are asked to choose from a broad and disparate number of courses to fulfill some basic general requirements without an eye on fundamental courses. Thus, in order to obtain a good education, students will need to design with the guidance of a mentor a worthwhile liberal arts curriculum. In the final analysis, students form their mind and will, even in less than favorable circumstances. In some cases, they need to take it on themselves to create their own curriculum in the western tradition of the liberal arts. This book intends to address in its different chapters how this can take place, that is, in whatever contexts students find themselves in the process and the content of forming their mind and will in the western tradition of the liberal arts.

Spending so much time, effort and money for a college education must serve some higher purpose: the cultivation of the soul and the service of others. This book will help students understand the real purpose of higher education, give practical advice on how this education might be obtained, and suggest ways in which a student can gain further benefit from these important years in college.

The education of one of the Founding Fathers, John Adams, indicates the value of a classical college education. In 1751, Adams went to Harvard College at the age of 16 where he obtained a good liberal arts education, including Latin. From there he went on to teach school in Worcester and, while he debated between studies in medicine and law, he read Milton, Virgil, Voltaire and Bolingbroke.[5] A few years later, he studied law with a lawyer in Worcester and began a distinguished career in law in Boston. His university studies enabled him to become a statesman and eventually president in the service of the nascent United States. Of note, his education had enlarged his mind and horizons. One interesting example was his reading habits. During his trips on horseback riding the court circuit, he carried in his saddlebags a copy of Cervantes' *Don Quixote.*[6]

---

[5] David McCullogh, *John Adams* (New York: Simon & Schuster, 2002), 39. Already as a boy, one of his earliest and proudest possessions was an edition of Cicero's *Orations.* Idem, 34.
[6] Idem, 69.

Recommended Reading:

John Henry Newman, *The Idea of a University.* University of Notre Dame Press, 1982.

David McCullough, *John Adams.* Simon & Schuster, 2002.

I. THE PURPOSE OF A UNIVERSITY EDUCATION

A university is a privileged place where professors and students come together to teach and to study with the objective of learning; they seek the cultivation of the soul: the intellect and the will. In addition to the necessary book-learning, students have the opportunity to examine reality and to foster a sense of wonder, asking and pondering on the "why" of things more than on the "how," so typical of modern natural sciences.

The pursuit of truth and virtue should be the goal of students and teachers alike. These objectives are countered by the generally accepted and unquestioned academic dogma of relativism, the idea that there is no one truth about things and reality. The other major obstacle is the lack of self-discipline and virtue. Students' newfound freedom and their lack of self-rule hinder them from seeking or accepting truths. Their moral life clouds their intellectual pursuit and acceptance of truth.

Already in the 4th century BC, Socrates (470-399 BC) and Plato (ca 428-348 BC) explored the human soul and its faculties or powers through which the soul comes to the knowledge of what is *real* and good. They explained how man must escape the shadow of things to come to the true knowledge of things. In *The Republic,* Plato established a hierarchy of virtues for life in society, at the top of which he placed justice.[7] His student Aristotle (384-322 BC) continued to study the make-up of *being* - the reality of things as we know them, arriving at the notion of matter and form. From a keen observation of the change in things, he distinguished different types of causality: material, efficient, formal and final. In his *Nichomachean Ethics,* he studied at length the ethical behavior of men and, in his *Politics,* their relationships in the working and governance of society.

Human beings have a fundamental need to find truth, beauty and goodness, and the university is the place where students should be

---

[7] For Plato there is something greater than justice and the other virtues; it *is To Agathon* (the good), and knowledge is concerned with the idea of the good. Eric Voegelin, *Order and History* (Vol. III)*: Plato and Aristotle*, (Louisiana: Louisiana State University Press, 1957).

able to learn what Socrates, Plato, Aristotle and other important philosophers have taught concerning these important matters. At the university, they should be helped to frame the most important questions about the meaning of life, suffering and how to live a virtuous life. These questions and answers are not to be found in the media and in today's other fast-paced communications. A university should be a place where they find the truth that leads to wisdom and virtue.

In addition to philosophy and theology, where the higher truths about *being* (metaphysics) and acting (ethics) are to be sought, the truth about specific things is found through many different sciences. John Henry Newman presented the picture of a university as a whole circle of learning. Students cannot pursue every subject that is open to them, but:

> "they will be the gainers by living among those and under those who represent the whole circle. This I conceive to be the advantage of a seat of universal learning, considered as a place of education. An assemblage of learned men, zealous for their own sciences, and rivals of each other, are brought, by familiar intercourse and for the sake of intellectual peace, to adjust together the claims and relations of their respective subjects of investigation. They learn to respect, to consult, to aid each other."[8]

In an environment of friendship, passion for truth and study, students can cultivate their minds and wills under men of learning, even though each one pursues one or a few sciences out of a multitude.

Newman used the word "cultivation" to refer to the formation of the mind;[9] in doing so, he consciously chose a precise English word.

---

[8] John H Newman, "Discourse 5: Knowledge its own end," in *Idea of a University* (London: Longmans, Green and Co, 1929), 101. This re-impression of an 1852 edition will be the one quoted.
[9] Newman focused on the formation of the intellect in his treatment of the university in the *Idea of a University*, but in his work at Oriel College in Oxford, the Catholic University of Ireland and the Oratory

Today most of us know little about cultivating land. Perhaps a grandfather or great uncle had some land that he farmed, but for the most part, we are unfamiliar with seeds, crops or barns. Cultivating land is a hard enterprise, a long, arduous and deliberate one ordered to the production of crops. It requires the proper soil and adequate water, good seed and knowledge of farming.

Education is no less difficult and important. It calls for a selection of candidates, good books, talented teachers, sufficient time and the proper environment. The mind, with its faculties, reason, imagination and memory, has to be cultivated or trained, beginning at an early age at home and later in grammar school. Without the proper training, the mind is like a barren field, a wasteland. On the other hand, with proper training and assistance, the mind is like a fertile field yielding a bountiful harvest. The fruit of this toil is learning, which is to the soul what food is to the body.

There are many social and sporting activities that take place at a university, but the real purpose of a university is the formation of the intellect. This education is often confused with book knowledge, learning many facts about many subjects. Education certainly involves reading, but primarily it is about developing habits of mind, primarily the capacity to understand arguments, analyze conclusions, make judgments, discriminate between ideas, grasp the parts of the whole and the relationships between the parts. Other habits include the ability to articulate ideas and to refute errors.

Based on an intellectual tradition independent of particular teachers, Newman wrote:

> "(The student) apprehends the great outlines of knowledge, the principles on which it rests, the scale of its parts, its lights and its shades, its great points and its little, as he otherwise cannot apprehend them. Hence it is that his education is called 'Liberal.' A habit of mind is formed which lasts through life, of which the attributes are freedom, equitableness, calmness, moderation, and wisdom; or what in a former Discourse I have ventured to call a philosophical habit. ."[10]

School in Birmingham he gave just as much importance to the formation of the will and the spiritual life.

Newman considered the formation of a habit of mind to be the main purpose of university with regard to students. It is "the special fruit of the education furnished at a University, as contrasted with other places of teaching or modes of teaching." This contrasts with other worthy enterprises such as trade schools, professional schools and places of training (or apprenticeship).

The best way to educate this habit of mind is by the study of liberal arts that began in Athens, the location of the first university which was comprised of a number of small schools of philosophy beginning in the 4th and 3rd centuries BC. The tradition continued in the medieval universities of Europe, beginning with the University of Bologna, Oxford, Paris, Cambridge, Salamanca, Cologne, Alcalá and others.

The liberal arts were seven subjects taught at all universities. The *Trivium*, Latin for "three ways," taught students to think in a systematic and critical way, enabling them to reason well and prepare for the subjects of the *Quadrivium*, Latin for "four ways," and other subjects. Every student who obtained a Bachelor of Arts degree studied the first three arts: (*Trivium*) - grammar (including literature), rhetoric and logic. Those who went on to obtain a Masters in the Arts studied four other liberal arts (*Quadrivium*) - mathematics, geometry, astronomy and music theory, in addition to Hebrew, Greek philosophy and history. Only some students went on to obtain a Masters degree and, even fewer, a Doctoral degree.

Learning grammar meant learning the rules of composition and reading comprehension with the use of the Sacred Scriptures as the text. The word "grammar," however, leads people mistakenly to equate this with the study of spelling and punctuation. It was much more. Students studied Latin (and other ancient languages) for a number of years. Students at the medieval universities learned the art of rhetoric by studying texts from famous orators like Cicero's *Treatise on Rhetorical Invention* and Aristotle's *Rhetoric*. They acquired skills in defending propositions and winning arguments, and developed the ability to persuade others through speech. This

---

[10] Ibid.

art focused on Christian rhetoric concerned more with religious truths than with legal cases, as in the Greek and Roman rhetoric.

The study of formal logic (Aristotelian logic) enabled them to analyze propositions and judgments, to refute erroneous conclusions and formulate correct syllogisms. Aristotle's treatises on logic served as the basis for this study.

This rigorous study of language and logic over the space of a number of years developed the habits of mind of the students. Scholarship at the University of Alcalá was such that in 1522 the university press published the Polyglot Bible in Latin, Hebrew and Greek. Alcalá became the center for the study of the humanist Erasmus of Rotterdam, and in 1525, the university press published one of Erasmus' books, *Enchiridion militis christiani* (*Handbook of a Christian Knight*).

In today's universities, the study of these and related subjects is called the Humanities, but the term is a general one that now includes many other subjects. The mandatory English comprehension and writing course for freshmen does not compare in any way to the formation given to students of liberal arts in former centuries. Nor do random courses on literature or history form properly the intellect of students. They acquire a lot of information but they are not able to understand it well, discriminate between one thing and another, or to place the facts into context. For this, students need a prior study of philosophy of *being* and philosophy of man. The reading of the so-called Great Books by themselves without adequate preparation and guidance is no guarantee for the training of the mind and sound judgment.[11]

Colleges and universities are the places best equipped for the formation of the mind because their focus is precisely on intellectual development, and they have many professors devoted to this task. In our times, however, the true purpose of colleges and universities - a

---

[11] Frederick D. Wilhelmsen made this point to be discussed in the following chapter in his provoking essay, "The Great Books, Enemies of Wisdom," *Modern Age* (1987): 323-331. Accessed November 10, 2014 www.mmisi.org/ma/31_3-4/wilhelmsen.pdf

liberal arts education - has been sacrificed to expediency, science and technology.

In general, universities fail to educate the minds of its students. Students learn many facts in many subjects. Many obtain practical work skills and most obtain some degree. However, they are ill prepared in making judgments and sound reasoning. Many are unable to articulate clear and convincing thoughts or to refute erroneous propositions. In a few words, they lack good habits of mind.

Learning for Learning's Sake

Underlying the reasons for the failure in education of universities is the pragmatism of contemporary Western culture that is counter to the primary purpose of learning - knowledge itself. People want tangible results that are readily noticeable and often translate into selfish monetary or other material gains. Now common throughout Western countries, the philosophy of pragmatism stands out in the United States where it found ready acceptance. Dickens points it out in his novel *Martin Chuzzlewit* in which the main character, upon arrival in the United States, finds out that what counts is making money. He runs into con artists who rob him of his money. Of course, it is a parody but, like every exaggeration, it holds some truths.[12]

We live in a country with many engineers and businessmen. So much of the development and wealth of the country is due to persons with these professions. They have specific talents for designing, building and commerce, all very important for the economy of a country. Unfortunately, however, those who pursue careers in these areas hardly study any humanities at the university. Undergraduates in these careers know a lot about building objects and businesses, but do not know about philosophy, theology, history and literature, and therefore do not develop the habits of mind proper to the liberal arts.

---

[12] Dickens criticized the no lesser corruption of English society with the portrayal of the dishonesty and avarice of Montague Tigg and Jonas Chuzzelwhit, characters in *Martin Chuzzlewit.* Charles Dickens, *The Life and Adventures of Martin Chuzzlewit* (London: Chapman & Hall, Ltd., 1868).

The problem with the study of the humanities at universities is that these subjects are not immediately useful. Engineering, business and all the empirical sciences take precedence in the curriculum, buildings and general view of education. This is the so-called problem of Useful Education, which was the subject of heated debate in 19th century England. The usefulness of the study of the classics, literature, history and other humanities was put into question. Stated succinctly: Are the humanities useful? And for what are they useful? An equally brief reply is that learning and the humanities are good in themselves, and they have an indirect usefulness to man and society. A person with a liberal arts education has deeper insights into human nature, unique perspectives of world events, diverse interests and the capacity to articulate these ideas so as to be perfectly understood, whether it be through a speech that inspires a nation, a novel that touches the heart or music that lifts the soul.

Learning is useful in itself because it perfects the mind. Each faculty is perfected when it attains its proper goal. We can say that the object of the intellect or reason is knowledge. The perfection of the soul and its faculties is a great good that is called excellence or magnanimity, which is greatness of the soul. In addition, it is rightly said that learning is for the sake of learning. Just as virtue is its own reward, so learning, too, is its own reward.

Newman articulated this idea in the following words:

> "I am asked what is the end of University Education, and of the Liberal or Philosophical Knowledge which I conceive it to impart: I answer, that what I have already said has been sufficient to show that it has a very tangible, real, and sufficient end, though the end cannot be divided from that knowledge itself. Knowledge is capable of being its own end. Such is the constitution of the human mind, that any kind of knowledge, if it be really such, is its own reward."[13]

He explained that "knowing" is a need felt by the soul. Men by nature wish and need to know the truth about things that make up reality.

---

[13] Newman, "Discourse 5: Knowledge its own end," 102-103.

In support of his assertion, Newman said of one of his favorite writers:

> "Hence it is that Cicero, in enumerating the various heads of mental excellence, lays down the pursuit of Knowledge for its own sake, as the first of them. 'This pertains most of all to human nature,' he says, 'for we are all of us drawn to the pursuit of Knowledge; in which to excel we consider excellent, whereas to mistake, to err, to be ignorant, to be deceived, is both an evil and a disgrace.'"[14]

When someone plays a sport - for instance, soccer - the person may have in mind various objectives, such as enjoyment, health, camaraderie, or winning a championship, but enjoyment itself is a very good reason for playing soccer. Without the other reasons it is sufficient reason for playing this sport. Something similar could be said about mountain climbing, playing musical instruments and a host of human activities. All of them may have a useful application, but in themselves, they are valuable if they perfect the person.

The learning proper for the cultivation of the mind requires many hours of study as well as times of leisure, understood as time and space to contemplate what one has heard and read and to discuss it with teachers and friends. Philosopher Josef Pieper wrote of leisure as this contemplation of reality. He asserts that one of the foundations of western culture is leisure:

> "That much, at least, can be learnt from the first chapter of Aristotle's *Metaphysics*. And even the history of the word attests the fact: for leisure in Greek is *skole,* and in Latin *scola,* the English 'school.' The word used to designate the place where we educate and teach is derived from the word, which means 'leisure.' 'School' does not, properly speaking, mean school, but leisure."[15]

---

[14] Idem, 104.

[15] Josef Pieper, *Leisure: the Basis of Culture*, trans. Alexander Dru, (New York: Pantheon Books, 1964), 4.

Pieper explains how today we live to work, but we should instead seek the opposite: work to have leisure as did the Greeks and Romans, so much so that in Greek everyday toil is *a-scolia*, and in Latin it is *neg-otium*.[16] He notes, "The Christian and Western conception of the contemplative life is closely linked to the Aristotelian notion of leisure,"[17] and the distinction between the *artes liberales* and *artes serviles* (servile work). In Antiquity, the latter, which today would be equivalent to useful work, was reserved to slaves. We know that both are necessary, but modern man has turned everything into work by measuring it according to its usefulness. This has led to a religion of work, which is an inhumane view of work. Scientific results, technology and business are all necessary for our society, but culture depends on a correct understanding of the world, the relationship between its parts to the whole and our purpose for existence. This comes only through reflection on our work and relationships, and contemplation of the world and its creator that arises from leisure.

Hand in hand with the formation of the intellect is the formation of the will. University life is a period to develop and grow in virtue or character strengths. For many college and university students this, however, is where they make serious mistakes. Schall explains that college can be a place where these errors are corrected - if there is self-knowledge and honesty, or magnified, if this is lacking.[18] In other words, college is a time to educate one's freedom and capacity for self-rule, so indispensable for seeking truth and finding true happiness.[19]

Other Ends of the University

There are many indirect or secondary effects of a university education. Among these, two stand out: preparation for gainful employment and the formation of a gentleman. The former will be

---

[16] Idem.
[17] Ibid, 5.
[18] James V. Schall, S.J., *A Student's Guide to Liberal Learning* (Delaware: ISI Books, 2000), 28.
[19] Jutta Burgraff, *Made for Freedom, Loving, Defending and Living God's Gift* (New York: Scepter Publishers, 2012).

discussed in other chapters. It is enough to say here that cultivation of the habits of mind prepare persons to work in many diverse occupations. Often this will require a specific education or training after finishing studies in liberal arts, but the person will already be equipped with the necessary tools for learning these and working well. The latter is the development of character traits found in a gentleman.

In *The Idea of a University,* Newman gave a now well-known definition of a gentleman. It was in fact the description of the type of an educated man held by Lord Shaftesbury: someone who is well-versed and polite, moderate in his expressions, and one who never inflicts pain on others. Erudition and science are the basis for this type of man. The gentleman is a scholar and philosopher. For Newman, however, the ideal was not this type of gentleman. He had in mind the Christian scholar and gentleman, inspired in the model of St. Paul, St. Francis de Sales and his own patron, St. Philip Neri.[20]

In 1856, on the opening of the university church in Dublin, he preached to students and faculty: "I wish the intellect to range with the utmost freedom, and religion to enjoy an equal freedom; but what I am stipulating for is, that they should be found in one and the same place, and exemplified in the same persons. (...) I wish the same spots [centers] and the same individuals to be at once oracles of philosophy and shrines of devotion."[21]

Lord Brougham who, following Lord Shaftesbury, wished to change the university curriculum of the schools in Great Britain to introduce new science courses and professions in the universities, held that more useful knowledge and more libraries would inevitably bring

---

[20] M. Katherine Tilman examines Newman's ideas about this in his Oratory Papers and the *Essay on Christian Development* before the *Idea of a University.* M. Katherine Tilman ,"A Rhetoric in Conduct: The Gentleman of the University and the Gentleman of the Oratory," *Newman Studies Journal.* 5:2(2008), 6-25.
[21] John H Newman, "Intellect, the Instrument of Religious Training," in *Sermons Preached on Various Occasions,* 13. Accessed on November 10, 2014.
http://newmanreader.org/works/occasions/sermon1.html

peace and progress for society. Newman gave a stunning and no less sarcastic reply to Brougham: "Quarry the granite rock with razors, or moor the vessel with a thread of silk; then may you hope with such keen and delicate instruments as human knowledge and human reason to contend against those giants, the passion and the pride of man."[22]

Today, despite the failure to produce the promised results with an exponential increase in the number of colleges and libraries, the same tune continues to play in the minds of many who think the problems of the world will be solved with more knowledge and more laptop computers.

Liberal education can produce a gentleman and a professional, but it does not make the Christian. It is the practice of human and supernatural virtues that forges character and brings about true peace and progress among men. Reflecting on truth, Benedict XVI wrote: "Truth is never just theoretical. [...] Truth means more than knowing. Knowledge of truth has as its goal knowledge of good. [...] The truth makes us good, and goodness is truth."[23] For a Catholic, truth translates into fairness, respect towards people and a genuine spirit of tolerance for others in their study and research. Newman thought that by setting up universities, the Catholic Church was uniting what men had separated: reason and faith.[24]

The real purpose of higher education is the cultivation of the mind and the formation of character. Both of these require a rediscovery of the liberal arts, the "lost tools of learning." As will be noted in the

---

[22] Newman, "Discourse 5: Knowledge, its own end," in *Idea of a University*, 121.
[23] Benedictus XVI, "Lecture by the Holy Father BENEDICT XVI at the University of Rome, La Sapienza," (lecture intended to be given in Rome on Jan. 18, 2007).
[24] "Here, then, I conceive, is the object of the Holy See and the Catholic Church in setting up Universities; it is to reunite things which were in the beginning joined together by God, and have been put asunder by man." Newman, "Intellect, the Instrument of Religious Training," 12-13. Retrieved from http://newmanreader.org/works/occasions/sermon1.html

next chapter, few universities offer good liberal arts programs to students, but those who wish to pursue this education can create "their curriculum" with the help of Student Guides, such as those published by the Intercollegiate Studies Institute, their own reading, and the help of mentors.[25] Some readers may think that these claims are exaggerated. This is so because sadly we have become used to university and college life dominated by professional schools, sports teams and a vast array of extracurricular activities.

At best, universities have become centers of advanced scientific research. Thus, we think that this is what a university is all about. There are merits to all these activities and programs, but the undergraduate who attends a college or university needs to develop the intellectual habits of mind, which are not to be found in a random choice of electives from a disparate offering of courses that fulfill general education requirements or from training in particular occupations. Higher education is something different. It is about acquiring a habit of mind, a vision of the whole and confidently pursuing truth, beginning with the most important questions in life.

---

[25] James V. Schall puts it this way: "The best place for any young man or woman today can be stated in two steps: 1) the step of self-discipline and 2) the step of a personal library; both of these together will yield that freedom which is necessary to escape academic dreariness and to discover the wonder of reality, of *what is.* Even at its best, of course, learning means we need a lot of help, even grace, but we are here talking about what we can do ourselves." Schall, *A Student's Guide to Liberal Learning,* 25.

Recommended Reading:

Dorothy L. Sayers. "Lost Tools of Learning," essay, 1947. Accessed November 10, 2014 www.gbt.org/text/sayers.html

Frederick D. Wilhelmsen. "The Great Books, Enemies of Wisdom" essay, 1987. Accessed on November 10, 2014, www.mmisi.org/ma/31_3-4/wilhemsen.pdf

James V. Schall, S.J. *A Student's Guide to Liberal Learning,* Intercollegiate Studies Institute, 2000.

II. A Crisis of Liberal Arts Education

Higher education has lost its primary goal: the cultivation of the intellect and will of its students. This is so because it has lost an understanding of itself and the unity of the sciences, something that only the liberal arts can provide. There has been a loss of the unity of knowledge, and of the search for objective truths. The result has been a fragmentation of learning and a failure to ask the fundamental questions. Teachers and students ask a lot of questions but usually very specific ones that do not respond to the deepest needs of man: the need for meaning.

The crisis of the university is a crisis of the liberal arts tradition, but more fundamentally it is a crisis about man's capacity to know truth. In *The Closing of the American Mind,* Professor Allan Bloom attributes this failure to the unexamined acceptance of cultural relativism and historicism.[26] He defines the latter as "the view that all thought is essentially related to and cannot transcend its own time."[27] For most of the 20th century, these have resulted in the acceptance of one sole virtue of primary education: tolerance or openness with the consequent rejection of the liberal arts (western thought). Students arrive at the university with one belief: that truth is relative. Bloom contrasts this relativism with a true openness to knowledge; hence, the reason for the title of his book *The Closing of the American Mind.*

Universities and colleges have become, for the most part, large or small entities that house many or some professional schools and departments. Despite more or less eloquent mission statements, there is no actual common purpose other than advancing the individual goals of each of these professional schools or departments. The unity of learning has become fragmented, and this is reflected in the learning students seek and find -specialized knowledge and practical knowledge.

---

[26] Allan Bloom, "Introduction: One Virtue," in *The Closing of the American Mind: How Higher Education has Failed Democracy and Impoverished the Souls of Today's Students*, (New York: Simon and Schuster, 1987), 25-43.
[27] Idem, 40.

However, there are exceptions to this statement. I would like to mention, albeit in passing, some institutions of higher learning I have had the opportunity to visit that I think do have a unitary vision of man and university education: the University of Dallas, Franciscan University at Steubenville, Christendom College, Thomas Aquinas College and my alma mater the University of Navarre. These are examples of schools that try to form the individual student as a whole person, keeping with the best of western thought and focusing on the teaching of undergraduates.[28]

Two Models of Core Curriculum

During the 20th century, the classical liberal arts tradition of learning was rejected as something impractical, and in the United States it was replaced with the concept of a core curriculum. Mark. C. Henrie explains the two models of this core curriculum that arose: the Western Civilization Survey courses and the Great Books programs.[29]

The first approach was *Western Civilization:* survey courses which sought to present the large picture of Western thought and history. General Education in Western Civilization was a required sequence of history courses taught at universities, which arose during the two world wars and lasted until it was rejected in the 1960's, although universities such as Columbia and Princeton continue to have it as an elective. Henrie writes, "This method had the advantage of providing an approach to one incarnation of the human whole, western

---

[28] There are other schools in United States that subscribe to this vision in theory and practice. Some of these can be found in the Newman Guide to Choosing a Catholic College. http://www.cardinalnewmansociety.org/TheNewmanGuide/Recommendedcolleges.aspx. Abroad, in addition to the University of Navarre, there are a number of schools such as the University of La Sabana (Bogotá), the Panamerican University (Mexico City), the University of Los Andés (Santiago de Chile) inspired by St. Josermaría Escrivá and Blessed Alvaro del Portillo, that combine a liberal arts education, professional schools and research.
[29] Mark. C. Henrie, *A Student's Guide to the Core Curriculum* (Delaware: ISI Books, 2000), 10-14.

civilization - its arts, literature, philosophy, politics and religion - understood *as a whole.* This approach also had the advantage of locating the individual in historical time, of taking history seriously."[30] When poorly taught, it became an indoctrination and unexamined praise of the excellence of American culture. According to Henrie, the secular academics that developed the *Western Civ.* curricula at universities such as Columbia understated the role of Christianity.

The other approach was the *Great Books* model, of which St. John's College in Annapolis, Maryland, is the best known. In this curriculum, great works of literature and philosophy are read and studied by the students in their original texts. Various objections have been made to this model, one being the lack of sufficient historical consciousness - the history of the authors and events surrounding the texts is not given enough importance. Another is that in these programs "the history of the West is not a history of answers, 'but a history of questions, *permanent questions*' that can never have conclusive answers."[31] Despite these possible flaws, Henrie holds that the *Great Books* curriculum is superior to the survey approach of *Western Civ.* Other institutions have developed this type of curriculum, such as the University of Chicago, the University of Notre Dame and Thomas Aquinas College.[32]

The crisis of the university can also be correlated to the sharp rise in empirical sciences. The German university model, which began in 1810 with the Humboldt University of Berlin, was established on the principle of the union of teaching and research in the work of the individual scholar or scientist. This research-oriented type of university became the model for universities in the United States in the first half of the 20th century, such as the Johns Hopkins University. With the development of new technology and a great number of discoveries, universities have become highly developed

---

[30] Ibid.

[31] Ibid.

[32] Some humanists complain about the legitimacy of the Great Books programs, defending recent scholarship reinterpreting the classics. Allan Bloom comments that, "In their reaction there is a strong element of specialist's jealousy and narrowness." Bloom, *The Closing of the American Mind*, 346.

research institutions in biology, molecular biology, chemistry, physics and engineering. The results-driven labs and grants have only made empirical research grow even more. Although there is theoretical research, the larger part is applied research with "useful results" for industry or medicine. This practical and results-oriented framework of teaching and research has altered radically the vision of the university and intellectual discourse, as well as the necessity for serious ethical considerations in research in the natural sciences. Many students who wish to work in science do not see the need or purpose for studying liberal arts, which for them lack objectivity and are simply a waste of time and money.

Although many schools retain the title of liberal arts colleges, there are only a few universities and colleges in the United States where students are formed in the liberal arts tradition. In Universities and so-called liberal arts colleges, there are, to be sure, liberal arts or humanities programs, but these are not the same. They do not seek a unified knowledge of reality or the great ideals and institutions of western civilization.

Allan Bloom, professor at the University of Chicago, notes that in the sixties universities were intent on removing requirements, while in the eighties they were busy trying to put them back which they attempted to do in two ways. The first and easier way was to make use of existing introductory courses in each of the general divisions of the university: natural sciences, social sciences and humanities. The students learn a little about many things and they find this to be a preliminary to the real learning. "Thus they desire to get it over with and get on with what their professors do seriously. Without recognition of important questions of common concern, there cannot be serious liberal education, and attempts to establish it will be but failed gestures."[33]

The failure of this motivated the second approach, which was the creation of composite courses with the collaboration of professors from various departments with titles such as "Man in Nature," "War and Moral Responsibility," and "Culture and the Individual." Although this required specialized professors to broaden their

---

[33] Idem, 343.

41

perspectives, according to Bloom, these courses faced "the danger of trendiness, mere popularization and lack of substantive rigor."[34] In the hands of the best professors, these courses can deal with the permanent questions, at least making students aware of them, and giving them some knowledge of the important works that deal with them. Bloom contends that this is often not the case and that the faculties do not perceive such courses as their real business.

In the further words of Bloom, "There is no organization of the sciences, no tree of knowledge."[35] There is not only an absence of the whole of learning, there is no hierarchy in learning, and the students are not presented with the most important questions and courses and texts that can help them find the right answers. Thus, the great majority of Liberal Art Colleges have lost their identity and reason for being, becoming a confusing composite of Studies Programs and Departments. Bloom adds that the unresolved intellectual problem of *what a university is* cannot be resolved by the administration.[36] This disarray of higher education is evident throughout the country and has led to even further pitfalls: the students design their own courses and curriculum. A study of one of the top liberal arts colleges confirms the extent of this current trend in education.

Study of a Top Liberal Arts College

In 2013, the National Association of Scholars published a study of Bowdoin College, renowned as one of the top United States liberal arts colleges. It discloses the disjointed and relativistic state of the education offered to students.[37] Harvey Mansfield, professor of political philosophy at Harvard, sums up the findings of this extensive one-year study. To begin with, Bowdoin like so many of

---

[34] Ibid.

[35] Idem, 337.

[36] Idem, 344.

[37] Peter Wood and Michael Toscano, "What Does Bowdoin Teach? How a Contemporary Liberal Arts College Shapes Students," *National Association of Scholar's Report* submitted April 3, 2013, accessed on November 10, 2014.
http://www.nas.org/images/documents/What_Does_Bowdoin_Teac h.pdf

America's colleges is wedded to political correctness rather than to the pursuit of knowledge. Bowdoin writes that it "claims to be 'inclusive,' open to all claims, yet it does not include conservatives."[38] Out of its 182 faculty members, only perhaps half a dozen are conservatives.

Students at Bowdoin must design an education based on their own goals, the college's vision and a few requirements. Mansfield explains;

> "Except for light requirements of distribution outside one's major and of concentration within it, requirements that have been lessened whenever the college stops to think about them, the student is free to choose. By this principle, all courses are treated by the college as equal, none more important, none necessary to or contributing more toward the 'liberal arts.' A liberal arts education, the study says, has become an education in liberating oneself from the liberal arts."[39]

Consequently, students choose courses on current topics or "topical courses" on the environment ("sustainability") or homosexuality, or "global citizenship," or multiculturalism. This reaches the absurd as in one of the courses, *Queer Gardens*, which failed due to lack of enrollment.[40]

All courses are considered of equal importance. Instead of survey courses aimed at teaching a subject matter, courses aim to show the

---

[38] Harvey Mansfield, "The Higher Education Scandal," *Real Clear Politics*, May 20, 2013, accessed November 10, 2014. http://www.realclearpolitics.com/articles/2013/05/20/the_higher_education_scandal_118473.html

[39] Mansfield, "The Higher Education Scandal," ibid.

[40] "Explores how the garden in Western literature and art serves as a space for desire. Pays special attention to the link between gardens and transgression. Reconsiders one of the founding myths of Western culture: the idea of a lost Eden." Accessed November 10, 2014 at http://www.bowdoin.edu/gay-lesbian-studies/courses/f12.shtml

relevance of a professor's specialty. As for teachers at Bowdoin, the college is not so much a body of teachers that teaches students, it is a research institution of "over-praised" undergraduate student researchers whose research is defended by political correctness.

The topical courses offered lack rigor despite claims of universal scope and interdisciplinary nature. "Topical courses are featured in programs called 'Studies,' such as Gender and Women's Studies, Gay and Lesbian Studies (separate from the preceding), Environmental Studies, and Africana Studies, that were founded explicitly as political advocacy for their constituents."[41] Other programs "such as Asian Studies and Latin American Studies, with apparently neutral names, are now concerned mainly with repudiating Western colonialism."

The results are not surprising: "without wisdom, without culture." Mansfield closes with a striking indictment:

> "Bowdoin's curriculum lacks the academic standards of excellence that conservatives mostly and mainly defend in academia with little or no help these days from liberals. It is conservatives who deplore and resist the brazen politicization of the classroom, the loss of the great books, indeed the disregard of greatness in general, the corruption of grade inflation, the cheap satisfactions of trendiness, the mess of sexual license, the distractions of ideology, the aggrandizement and servility of administrators, the pretense and dissembling of affirmative action, the unmanly advice of psychologists, the partisan nonsense of professional associations, and the unseemly subservience everywhere to student opinion. None of these was necessary or useful in order to welcome those non-WASPs previously excluded from our colleges."[42]

This summary by Mansfield mirrors that of Bloom's almost thirty years earlier.[43] The experience of many students and professors on

---

[41] Ibid.
[42] Ibid.
[43] Bloom, *The Closing of the American Mind,* 337, 346.

college and university campuses throughout the United States confirms the findings of the Bowdoin study, leading to the conclusion that its findings can be generalized to the liberal arts colleges of the United States. How then can students obtain an undergraduate education in the Western tradition of liberal arts? It seems highly improbable but this is not the case. The rest of this chapter will address the possibility of realizing the goal of a university education given the landscape of today's higher education.

Only a small number of students will be able to attend one of the few colleges in the country that have good programs teaching western thought and civilization or studying the great texts. These are fortunate students who will find a community of teachers and fellow students with whom to develop a philosophical habit of mind and explore the best of Western thought and culture.

The rest of the students - the great majority of students - who wish to form their mind and will, seeking and finding answers for their questions in the intellectual tradition of the West, can still obtain a liberal arts education. However, they need to create their own curriculum in the western tradition following some aspects of the traditional seven liberal arts. In the departments of universities and colleges of the United States, students can still find courses that explore the central themes of the western tradition and that study the great texts.

This goal requires good advice and planning prior to beginning higher education because college student advisors and course catalogs do not point out these courses to students. Students need the proper understanding of the purpose of higher education and the liberal arts tradition, and an institution such as the Intercollegiate Studies Institute articulates this vision and offers concrete guidance. When students, with the help of such guides, create their own curriculum, they are actually choosing a classical "core curriculum" that embodies the wisdom and achievement of western thinkers. Their goal must be discovering the truth of things and becoming a civilized man or woman.

Such a curriculum was not something of the distant past. Philosophy professor and novelist Ralph McInerny recalled his studies at a minor seminary in Minnesota during 1942-45: "The curriculum was classical - Latin from the very beginning, Greek starting in the Third Year, English, history, math, science of a sort, and French or German."[44] McInerny wrote for the school newspaper and with others put on plays. He wrote of his teachers who were priests:

> "Among them were some of the best teachers I ever had. Classics were at the heart of the curriculum. In Latin, after a year of grammar, we read Caesar, went on to Cicero, and then to Virgil and Horace. I was tortured in Catullus by Father Walter Peters, a vain and eccentric man shaped like the letter S, a German among so many Irish. He also taught me Horace and inspired me to read Thomas Mann."[45]

Indeed, until the 1950's a student's core requirements consisted of more than half of his college coursework.[46] This has sadly changed. Now students spend a large amount of time fulfilling general requirements, without any substantial unity or rigor, and the requirements of their "major" or "concentration." This is even more reason for them to choose their electives carefully. Henrie provides students with detailed advice and a bibliography for a good classical core curriculum.[47]

In the *Student's Guide to the Core Curriculum,* he presents a core curriculum that consists of eight elective courses that students should take throughout their four years of undergraduate studies:

---

[44] Ralph McInerny, *I Alone Have Escaped to Tell You: My Life and Pastimes,* (South Bend: University of Notre Dame Press) 2011, 15.
[45] Idem, 16.
[46] Myra Harada, "History of Higher Education Curriculum," (Unpublished manuscript, 1994), 19-25. Retrieved on November 10, 2014. http://files.eric.ed.gov/fulltext/ED379977.pdf
[47] The Intercollegiate Studies Institute has prepared monographs from distinguished scholars offering more in detail reflections and advice on courses within different majors.

classical literature, ancient philosophy, the Bible, Christian thought before 1500, Modern Political theory, Shakespeare, United States History before 1865, and 19th Century European Intellectual History. This core curriculum takes into account the university's requirement of courses in sciences and a foreign language. This list does not pretend to be comprehensive, and at the end of the guide Henrie offers ten other elective courses that would complete the view of the Western *whole*. Among these are Comparative Literature, Music Appreciation and Art History, which should really be counted among the first group.

Some words on the study of music and fine arts are opportune here. A meaningful university education should include the study of basic music theory and history. This study should focus on classical Western music but include music from other civilizations as well. This education develops appreciation for beauty, which enriches the person and society in various ways, beginning with greater sensibility and respect for people. Many schools offer music courses for non-music majors but relatively few students take these courses, among other reasons because they do not see an immediate "usefulness." In addition there are many good books and recordings for the study of music. *Listen* is a complete course by musicologists Joseph Kerman and Gary Tomlinson, which includes many illustrations and recordings.[48] Another good course for more advanced students is *How to Listen and Understand Great Music* by musicologist Robert Greenberg.[49]

Something similar should be said about the importance of the study of painting and sculpture, art forms that exist since prehistoric times. The beliefs and sentiments of human beings have found expression in the fine arts and have contributed to the creation of the cultures of different civilizations. Besides the delight that art often produces in the observer, it teaches persons to understand people and cultures. There is also an important connection between aesthetic perception and the spiritual life. Appreciation for art cultivates the capacity for

---

[48] Joseph Kerman, Gary Tomlinson, *Listen,* 6th edition, Boston, Bedford/St. Martin's, 2008.
[49] Robert Greenberg, *How to Listen to and Understand Great Music,* 3rd edition, Chantilly, Virginia: The Teaching Company, 2006.

observation and fosters a contemplative attitude that opens the person to beauty, truth and goodness. Looking at good art can also deepen a person's ability to understand suffering and show empathy. Furthermore religious art, a frequent subject of art, not only can teach students religious beliefs, it can inspire them to develop a spiritual life (their relationship with God).

The Oxford History of Western Art is a good survey of western art with contributions by many art historians.[50] But even more than good courses students' love of music and the fine arts is awakened by visits to art museums and live musical performances. At most schools students can participate in a variety of singing groups and choirs, and in the larger ones they can play in or listen to orchestras and small group string ensembles.

As noted above choosing the right courses is also essential in gaining a good liberal arts education. In addition to the advice to be found in articulations of a good core curriculum, students need to read between the lines in course offerings. Courses that refer to a revision of the past, gender themes or esoteric subjects are suspicious and usually highly biased. It is unlikely that a course titled "Shakespeare's Sisters: Representing Women in the Renaissance" can offer an undergraduate a meaningful understanding of Shakespeare. A course titled "Shakespeare, Sex and Power" probably reduces the themes dealt by Shakespeare even if these two are important ones. Bloom notes:

> "There is an enormous difference between saying, as teachers once did, 'You must learn to see the world as Homer or Shakespeare did,' and saying, as teachers now do, 'Homer and Shakespeare had some of the same concerns you do and can enrich your vision of the world.' In the former approach, students are challenged to discover new experiences and reassess old; in the latter, they are free to use the books in any way they please."

---

[50] *The History of Western Art,* Martin Kemp, ed, Oxford: Oxford University Press, 2000.

Titles that indicate debunking of earlier truths are also likely to be very one-sided accounts of the subject. Survey courses in general, no matter their deficiencies, are better than specialized courses in history, literature and other subjects. For example, a course as specific as "Black Feminist Literary Traditions" might more properly be the subject for a graduate seminar. Students need a firm grounding in the main authors, their arguments and texts, and to examine the questions they asked and the context in which they lived. A quick search of a professor's publications and reading a chapter of one of his books can provide information about the content of his courses.

Choosing the right professors is also paramount for a good liberal arts education. A professor is a guide to truth. He or she is someone from whom to learn the path to follow, a person whom one can and should admire for his or her knowledge, integrity and genuine concern. The great Western model is Socrates who helped Plato and his other students to reason, always seeking the truth despite the cost. Confucius considered the teacher-student relationship as one of the five fundamental relationships. A teacher offers wisdom to students and, in turn, students show their respect, gratitude and loyalty. This type of relationship is analogous to the classical doctor-medical student relationship enshrined in the Hippocratic Oath. Students should thus seek out the good teachers. They should look for teachers that are respected for their academic rigor - not their capacity to entertain - and their respect for students. They should avoid the "easy" teachers or the ones known for their sophistry. A good professor remains a lifetime teacher and friend.

As important as choosing the teachers and courses for a college education is choosing and fostering meaningful friendships - another subject to be referred to in other parts of this book. Our colleges and universities are plagued with an anti-intellectualism that is due to a superficial and materialistic culture where sports and future material gain are set on high pedestals. The soul needs intellectual friendships that will nurture its growth and enlarge its views and understanding. Reading for courses and other reading should naturally lead to engaging dialogues. These sincere and probing conversations will spur men and women to a greatness of soul, the magnanimity about which Aristotle wrote. Referring to his years at a minor seminary, McInerny wrote, "It is in the nature of such schools, perhaps all schools, that much of one's learning takes place independently of classes and teachers (...) In short, we were taught, but we also educated one another and ourselves."[51]

In these conversations, among themselves and with their peers, students will ask the most important questions in life - questions about truth, about God, human relationships, justice, the meaning of suffering, etc. - and they will find answers in the accumulated wisdom of men and women, especially in classical western civilization and the Judeo-Christian West. They will see knowledge as a connected *whole*, instead of a fragmented assortment of contradicting truths, and they will learn to appreciate the centrality of religious belief and morality.

Only this type of education with mentors and peers will open the minds of students in America and elsewhere. Newman held that the liberal arts have the capacity "to open the mind, to correct it, to refine it, to enable it to know, and to digest, master, rule, and use its knowledge, to give it power over its own faculties (...)[52]

The crisis of the university, which is a crisis of the liberal arts, will not be solved in our times but it lies in the hands of the future professors and university presidents who are today's students. Now as in ages past, the pursuit of truth, goodness, beauty and justice requires the study of liberal arts that students can still attain if they think about the purpose of a university education, choose the right teachers and courses and form a good community of friends.

---

[51] Ralph McInerny, *I Alone Have Escaped to Tell You: My Life and Pastimes,* 18.
[52] Newman, "Discourse 5: Knowledge, its own end," *Idea of a University,* 122.

50

Recommend Reading:

Allan Bloom, "Introduction: One Virtue," in *The Closing of the American Mind: How Higher Education has Failed Democracy and Impoverished the Souls of Today's Students*, Simon & Schuster, 1987, 25-43.

Mark. C. Henrie, *A Student's Guide to the Core Curriculum*, Intercollegiate Studies Institute, 2000.

III. Choosing the Right College

To begin this chapter we must repeat an unpopular and sometimes uncomfortable truth: not everyone has the interest, the capacity or the need for a college education. Some people have special talents in music or sports that lead them to pursue directly a career path without studying at a college or university. There are many other paths to follow after a high school education in a variety of service industries, manual or skilled labor and small business enterprises. Higher education has become an over-priced and over-subscribed path that often falls short of its real ends and leaves students and families in significant debt.

Choosing the right college or university is a very important decision with lifelong consequences. There a person will grow and develop intellectually and morally. There he or she will form strong ties of friendship that will last a lifetime. There he or she will often meet his or her future spouse and find persons with whom to work on common projects and interests for many years. After four years, the school chosen will have become an *alma mater*, his or her second mother.

The choice of a college or a university really begins in junior year of high school or earlier. Senior year of high school is the time for applying to schools and qualifying in them. During this year, a short list is drawn up from the schools extending acceptances and weighed with information of the financial aid offered. Thus, the senior year is an operational year, but the more important work is done in junior year.

Something analogous should be said about the attitude required in high school in order to obtain a good foundation in liberal arts. This attitude should be exercised beginning in junior year or even earlier. It is a time for thinking about how to grow in the intellect and the will. Students should apply some of the principles suggested in this book for obtaining a liberal arts education in college but without waiting for college.

This translates into learning to write sentences and paragraphs well, improving the skill for analyzing a text, reading Shakespeare, acquiring a sense of history, and appreciating the fine arts. Students should not wait until college to begin to do this. They must exert themselves in English composition, literature, history, languages, and philosophy and theology courses if these are available to them. They should also take advantage of Advanced Placement courses offered in high schools.

A prestigious university may not always be the right choice. The economist Ernst F. Schumacher (1911-1977) tells in *A Guide for the Perplexed* of his going to Oxford as a young man, thinking that it was the greatest university of his time.[53] He was disappointed to find that what was taught had little bearing on the truth and the weightier questions of life. This critique does not disqualify Oxford but it indicates how even famous universities have lost touch with serious issues affecting students and the great philosophical and religious minds throughout history.

In deciding upon the best place to study, a candidate - as well as his or her parents - has to have a clear sense of the purpose of higher education. In this book, we have considered the principal objectives of a university education: the cultivation of the mind and the will. Whatever extracurricular activities a student elects, these must be just that: "*extra curriculum activities*" that do not detract from the very purpose of going to college or university. This is no easy task; it requires clear thinking and determination.

This chapter deals in general with the choice of a college or university. The choice of a school with a good liberal arts college or one with a good liberal arts program is discussed in an earlier chapter on the crisis of the liberal arts. The presumption here is that most students will go to neither and thus will need to create their own core curriculum if they seek to develop a good intellectual habit of mind in the tradition of the liberal arts.

In part, this chapter could be summed up by stating reasons that should not determine the choice of a particular college, namely, a beautiful campus with many sports fields, a nationally known sports

---

[53] See James V. Schall, *A Student's Guide to Liberal Learning* (Delaware: ISI, 2000), 12-13.

team, the reputation of a party school, a prestigious name, an ideal location or one attended by some friends. Except for perhaps the last two motives, these are weak reasons to invest one's youth and family fortune in a given school.

It is true that a dedicated and clever student can learn anywhere and that every school has at least a few good professors and fellow students, but this is poor consolation for choosing a school for a superficial reason. The intellectual, moral, spiritual, artistic and historic milieu of a given place creates the *genius loci* or the 'enchantment of a location.' Newman could say that of the Oxford of his day or the Sorbonne (Paris) of the Middle Ages. If one can choose and afford a better place to study, why settle for a lesser one? In the right environment, a person's talents and interests blossom.

Personal Objectives

Besides recognizing the fundamental reasons for going on to higher education, a person needs to establish and clarify educational objectives. Every person should establish the habit of having some short-term, mid-range and long-term objectives to guide his thoughts and actions. These objectives mature with time; they are refined and corrected, and sometimes changed altogether. They serve as a guide and help rather than as a strict rule.

The short-term objectives are those goals that may vary from week to week or month to month which ensure a good use of time. Examples would be reading a certain book, writing an essay, visiting a sick person or repairing a damaged object. The mid-term objectives are usually goals that take time to accomplish and often depend on other objectives or circumstances. These entail planning, including various short-term objectives. Examples would be organizing and running a tutoring program, learning a language, or improving the capacity to speak in public.

These types of objectives should be subordinated to long-term objectives, which can involve a number of years, many years, or even a lifetime. The latter are the types of goals that students in the upper years of high school should be encouraged to ponder. The people around them whom they admire, or the heroes about whom they read, can awaken desires of objectives to accomplish in life. Here good biographies and novels often serve as an inspiration. The lives of accomplished persons and the descriptions of their careers sow in youth the desire to be one type of person or another, to study in a given college or university, and maybe the desire to practice a given profession in the distant future.

Students who have developed such a habit of setting goals learn in high school to think about the future and to dream of their future endeavors in life. They have not lived in a world of make-believe, playing video games for hours on end or binge-watching television. Even if the latter were the case, before going to college a person needs to sit down and think about his or her future and to speak with close friends, parents and teachers about possible choices. It is often very helpful to write down one's thoughts and to look again at them periodically to make revisions or corrections.

As explained in the preceding chapters, college students should study subjects that help them to develop a habit of mind without seeking to focus on the study of one profession early on in their undergraduate studies. This would hamper and narrow their intellectual formation. Still, this is not contrary to the interests and attention paid to long-term educational goals, which some students have at an early age. When students have such goals, this facilitates their choice of a school whether at home or even abroad, in the case of a very particular interest. Long-term goals can reinforce the study of languages, music, math or some other subjects that would help them achieve these future plans.

Selection Criteria

Whether or not students have good self-knowledge and future plans when applying for colleges and universities, they need to have selection criteria to narrow down the number of schools to which they should apply. The College Board, a nonprofit organization, suggests that five to eight applications are sufficient for most students to find acceptance into a "suitable institution," depending naturally on the student's personal record and circumstances.[54] It is

---

[54] "How Many Applications are Enough?" CollegeBoard

common nonetheless for students to send applications to a larger number of schools. There are some general criteria that are important in choosing possible schools to consider or visit. Without adequate reflection, people can easily visit a school and consider it as a place of future study because the school is known for one of its sports teams or because family members or friends have studied there.

The popular U.S. News & World Report Ranking of Colleges ranks schools based on some academic outcomes. It gives a lot of weight to indicators such as graduation and freshmen retention rates. Although schools are divided into categories, including liberal arts, the above mentioned indicators and others such as faculty resources, student selectivity and alumni giving do not measure the intellectual and moral education of students or indicate the quality of the liberal arts education offered. It is hard to measure this but it can be equally misleading to think that a listing of schools can provide students and parents with the type of information that they need.

Before looking at some positive criteria, it is good to remember again some, so to speak, negative criteria - reasons not to choose a college. It is easy to make poor choices based on outward appearances. A school with many new buildings including good sports facilities and green lawns may or may not be a good college. A university with a top NCAA basketball team may have a lot of student camaraderie surrounding the school team; it also has a lot of excessive alcohol consumption, and a good amount of superficial conversations and activities surrounding sports.[55]

---

http://professionals.collegeboard.com/guidance/applications/how-many
This article notes that, "This number should be made up of a combination of 'safety,' 'probable' and 'reach' colleges," where "safety" means little likelihood of rejection of the applicant, and "reach" is the student's top choices but have little likelihood of acceptance.
[55] National Institute of Health, "Heavy drinking in College Students: Who is at risk and what is being done about it?" *Journal of General Psychology,* 133(2006): 406-9.

The academic life of an institution is paramount, yet for a student or parent it is often hard to make a judgment, especially given the number of schools that exist. College and University guides can be helpful, as well as advice from alumni of the schools under consideration regarding the intellectual life of different schools. Good institutions of higher education sponsor recognized annual conferences or special events that draw visiting scholars and students. Some are distinguished as the origin of intellectual movements or discoveries made by faculty members.

It is of interest to ask about a school's outstanding professors and to inquire about their most distinguished accomplishments. It is important to know if these professors actually teach undergraduates or if most of the teaching is done by graduate student teachers. Just as important is the need to find out about the climate of intellectual honesty and freedom exercised by the professors towards the students. Basically, are professors or departments wed to certain ideologies? Is there respect for students and their views?

A second selection criterion for a college or university is the general state of the institution's moral and spiritual life. Newman argued in favor of respect for the freedom of students' decisions regarding religious practice. He decried a purely formal attendance to religious services, and especially by students who had been drunk the night before. Just the same, he lived with high moral standards and encouraged students to do likewise. The Newman Guide to Catholic Colleges helps students and parents identify schools in which religion and student life are taken seriously on the part of the administration. Student newspapers are a good gauge of the moral environment of a school. Although egregious immorality sadly exists in most college campuses, some schools have a reputation for it, and some school administrations go out of their way to establish not only co-ed dorms but co-ed bathrooms. A Catholic college that insists on these types of living arrangements and endorses all types of sexual promiscuity is probably not worth attending.[56]

---

[56] B.J. Willoughby, J.S. Carroll, "The impact of living in co-ed resident halls on risk-taking among college students," *Journal of American College Health.* 58(2009):241-6.

The state of the Catholic Chaplaincy or other Christian Student Centers is a good indication of the religious life of the institution. Many schools with Christian origins live off of past prestige and association with once vibrant religious orders. The activities promoted on the websites and bulletin boards, and confession schedule, or lack thereof, provide an idea of the spiritual climate of the religious centers that is so vital for the moral and spiritual needs of students.

Finances

A third important criterion for the selection of a school is the financial cost. For some families this is not a major issue but for most it is, and a very important one. For the 2011–12 academic year, annual current dollar prices for undergraduate tuition, including room and board, were estimated to be $14,300 at public institutions, $37,800 at private nonprofit institutions, and $23,300 at private for-profit institutions.[57] Students are not used to making long-term financial considerations so they must be helped to understand that student loans of large amounts are a heavy burden that will make other commitments, such as marriage, having children and the acquisition of a home, difficult. They have to consider future job opportunities and the amount of time it will take them to repay these debts.

There is a host of financial aid offered by schools, the complexity of which requires the assistance of university financial aid officers. Despite the many forms of federal, state and private aid, the majority seems to be in the form of student loans. At present, the student debt in the US is $1.1 trillion, according to the *Economist,* more than America's credit card debt.[58] And 15% of the students default on these debts within three years. The latter statistic serves as a

---

[57] U.S. Department of Education, National Center for Education Statistics. (2013). Digest of Education Statistics, 2012 (NCES 2014-015), Chapter 3.
[58] "Making College Cost Less," *The Economist,* online April 5, 2014; http://www.economist.com/news/leaders/21600120-many-american-universities-offer-lousy-value-money-government-can-help-change

cautionary note that advises more careful planning on the part of students and parents.

When students have very good academic records and many talents, they can often receive merit scholarships and therefore the financial criterion is of less importance.

Families with financial needs can obtain scholarships for their children but these are usually insufficient to cover most of the cost for room and board, no less tuition. To qualify the combined family income must be $50,000 or less, practically poverty level, often with no consideration for the size of family sharing that income. Despite adjustments for the number of children enrolled in college, the difficulty is even greater when more than one son or daughter is in college. Some Ivy League schools accept students and afterwards determine their financial needs, giving them all the assistance that they need. However, this applies to a relatively small number of candidates for higher education.

Because of the financial consideration, the great majority of students must go to state colleges or universities where the average tuition and board is lower than at private schools. Students still need to seek financial aid in scholarships and student loans. They must be prepared to work during the summers and Christmas holidays to earn some money to pay for part of their expenses.

For the same reason many students who wish to continue with higher education attend city and community colleges where they obtain associates degrees and afterwards transfer to four-year schools to obtain bachelor's degrees.

Among students seeking sports scholarships to attend college, some do so for love of the sport at which they excel and others as a way to pay for school. Although the first is understandable, unless someone acts for the latter reason, it is unlikely that his or her years in school will be fruitful in terms of gaining a good college education. Needless to say, it is very difficult to play team sports in college and do good academic work. Some students are able to do so but it takes clear ideals and determination. It is likely that many graduate after four years of playing sports on a scholarship, without obtaining a good liberal education or a degree that will help them find employment.[59]

Higher education has always been expensive although the costs have risen significantly in the last decades for various reasons, including the construction of costly buildings, science labs and libraries as well as sports facilities, and the growth of faculties.[60] Although the cost of higher education is almost a deterrent, anyone with a desire to pursue the cultivation of the mind and the will in a university should seek the advice and help of people and institutions to achieve his or her aim. It may require starting at a community college or working some years before starting his or her higher education. It may also entail studying and working part-time. Many people have done this before and others will continue to do it for the sake of a college degree.

Other Considerations

There are other considerations in making decisions to attend one school or another - naturally beginning with acceptance - that people take into account. Sometimes personal or family health concerns or work motives will dictate studying and living in a given city. Personal relationships may also affect decisions concerning relocation for studies. For these and other motives, each candidate and his or her

---

[59] Chris Amos, "Athletic Involvement and Academic Achievement," *Digital Commons @ Liberty University.* (2013). Retrieved on October 5, 2014. http://digitalcommons.liberty.edu/cgi/viewcontent.cgi?article=129 0&context=masters; Michael T. Maloney and Robert E. McCormick, *The Journal of Human Resources.* 28(1993):555-570. An examination of the role that intercollegiate athletic participation plays in academic achievement: Athletes' feats in the classroom,
[60] "Much of this cash has been wasted on things that have nothing to do with education—plush dormitories, gleaming stadiums and armies of administrators. In 1976 there were only half as many college bureaucrats as academic staff; now the ratio is one to one." The Leaders, "Making College Cost Less."

family need to establish an individually tailored list of criteria for selection of schools.

Another consideration that comes into play is the size of a school. Some students are fine at large institutions while others feel lost or unhappy in the large and often impersonal environment of state universities. Each person has to know himself or herself and determine where he or she flourishes best.

Lastly, a visit to schools, when possible, can make certain impressions on candidates that change their previous desires. Again, students and parents should be careful about being persuaded by a beautiful campus or the mention of some Nobel Prize laureates on the faculty of a school. Rather, they need to sit in on some classes, ask upper class students what they think of their school, and observe the student life and climate of the Newman Center.

Deliberation and Decision Making

After having decided on some sort of selection criteria and having looked into many schools, a student and often his family need to narrow down the number of schools to which he will apply. The application process is time consuming and expensive. Once a student is accepted into some schools, he or she has to deliberate and come to a decision. While throughout this process it is important to have sought advice from friends, teachers and professionals, once it comes to a final decision, it is just as important to continue to seek good advice.

Certainly, the decision one makes is not irrevocable. Sometimes, after a year or more, a student will need to change schools for a host of reasons, such as personal or family ones. At other times, the academic environment or student life is not what he expected. This too is part of learning and making decisions due to changes in life or mistakes. Starting again at another college can be a good occasion to begin afresh, but it will also require a more concerted effort to make the right choice.

Prayer too is necessary to make the right school and career decisions. Beginning with the years in high school and even earlier, a student should pray to God for guidance, and when it comes to making the choice of a college and embarking on this time of study and maturing as person, daily prayer becomes even more necessary.

Acceptance to one's school of choice and the decision to study there is usually the result of a long and difficult process and yet it is only the start of higher education with all its opportunities and obligations in the intellectual and moral life. By means of conversations and the clarification of objectives and ideals, a student can come to the best decision possible, making a choice for the school that will become his *alma mater,* the place where he will develop the necessary habits of mind and strengths of character for his life and form lasting relationships.

Recommended Reading:

Choosing the Right College, An ISI guide 2014-2015.

Joseph A. Esposito. *The Newman Guide to Choosing a Catholic College,* 2015. Delaware: ISI Books, 2014.

VI. GOD IN THE UNIVERSITY CLASSROOMS

God is absent from most college and university classrooms of North America and Europe. He was expelled by the administrators and teachers. This is a strange 20th century phenomenon that had already taken place in large measure at Yale University by 1950 as documented by William Buckley in *God and Man at Yale*.[61] Today in many universities, except for philosophy and theology classes, it is taboo to speak about God in classrooms except to repeat Nietzsche's cry: "God is dead," or not relevant. The one who actually died, and after a period of insanity, was the philosopher. God is very much alive. He is a perfect Spirit, the creator of the Universe, in existence before the creation of time and space.

The strangeness of the reversal of this situation lies in the fact that the forerunners of modern universities were institutions where all the students studied about God and his attributes. Philosophy and theology were central subjects of study and deliberation. The reading of the *Sacrae Paginae*, the Holy Scriptures, was the basis for much of this study. Although based on a common faith, the pursuit of truth fostered inquiry and debate. In Paris, Oxford, Salamanca and other early universities, there were serious theological debates on questions concerning God's attributes, the human soul and the sacraments.

The advent of modern science and its rapid development coupled with its practical applications led to the removal of philosophy and theology from their privileged place. The inductive method of reasoning proper to the empirical sciences gained ascendancy over the deductive method of theology. This gradual change accelerated in the early 20th century. Some decades earlier, the historical critical method in both historical research and literature had put in doubt the historicity of the Old and New Testament.

A great number of colleges and universities in the United States originated as Christian institutions. Seven of the eight Ivy League schools had religious affiliations and some were Protestant

---

[61] William F. Buckley, *God and Man at Yale: the Superstitions of 'Academic Freedom'*. Washington D.C.: Regnery Publishing, 1951.

seminaries. Harvard, Yale, Princeton and Brown pride themselves in their pluralistic views, which is to say atheistic or agnostic culture with tolerance for Eastern religions and a soft Christian sentimental religion. William Buckley describes the state of religious education in the late 40's at Yale, which was contrary to the desire of its alumni espoused agnosticism and socialist views on the economy. He noted how religion was ridiculed or, even worse, ignored and brushed aside as insignificant. It was reduced to the same importance as an elective course in a foreign language. What he accurately diagnosed over sixty years ago has become widespread in the private and public institutions of higher education. Methodist and other Christian schools became secularized, losing their mission and thus blending with the rest of the colleges and universities, out of a desire to accommodate the aggressive secular culture; a culture that, for all of its talk of openness and tolerance, is actually one of power and dominance over reason. In an effort to pursue autonomy, they actually became conformists.

As Buckley explained, the way God and religion are portrayed in many biology, economics, psychology, history and literature courses gives an unfair and inaccurate presentation of religious truths and practices. Most young undergraduates are surprised by attacks made in class by the professors. They are not prepared to respond to them, even less in the intimidating way the claims are presented by professors. A typical argument in biology courses would run like this: the soul cannot be proven under a microscope, thus it cannot exist, or at best, it is an explanation for religious emotions. A similar argument, a favorite of a Princeton biology professor, is the following: chimpanzees and humans have 98% of the same chromosomes, thus humans are just like chimpanzees. We may derive from a common ancestor, but the human soul accounts for a big difference: human beings write sophisticated plays, worship God in magnificent temples and reflect on their own behavior and thoughts in lengthy treatises. In history courses, the Catholic Church is discredited for the Crusades, the Inquisition and Galileo's imprisonment. Never mind the facts, the explanations and the truth. The Church is found guilty before the facts are examined. Everyone knows that it did evil and that it should pay for it.

Fortunately, there are fair-minded professors at public universities who respect the religious beliefs of their students. A friend had two professors at the University of Florida who were not Catholic but they took seriously academic freedom and respected the dignity of each student to pursue truth. One was a History professor who helped my friend discover truth through the beauty of the Medieval Catholic culture and the passionate defense of beliefs during the Reformation. Another professor who taught religion had great open-ended discussions with his student on grace, works, Luther and the sacraments. He encouraged students to study and go deeper into their religious beliefs.[62] Many more professors like these are needed in our colleges and universities.

Catholic schools, including some of the earliest schools of higher education in the United States, such as Georgetown University, Boston College and Notre Dame, are different because in these schools theology continues to be taught. These universities have departments of theology and chapels in which the Mass is celebrated. Nonetheless, in many Catholic schools, a large part of the faculty is non-Catholic, and many of these faculty members are nonbelievers. There are professors who are respectful of religion and of the mission of a Catholic university, but there are others who question and ridicule religion with the implicit toleration of department heads under the guise of academic freedom.

In the 1990's, Pope John Paul II sought to restore the Christian identity of Catholic institutions of higher learning through the Apostolic Constitution *Ex Corde Ecclesiae.* The Pope reminded the university authorities that they should maintain the Catholic identity of a university through the recruitment of teachers and personnel who will further this goal. As for teachers, the constitution reads: "In ways appropriate to the different academic disciplines, all Catholic teachers are to be faithful to, and all other teachers are to respect, Catholic doctrine and morals in their research and teaching."[63] It

---

[62] Conversation with Daniel Hoffman, October 22, 2014. Daniel has a few children studying at State Universities.
[63] John Paul II, *Ex Corde Ecclesiae* [Apostolic Constitution on Catholic Universities], PartIIArt.4§3, accessed November 10, 2014, http://www.vatican.va/holy_father/john_paul_ii/apost_constitutions

specified further that: "In order not to endanger the Catholic identity of the University or Institute of Higher Studies, the number of non-Catholic teachers should not be allowed to constitute a majority within the Institution, which is and must remain Catholic."[64] Many teachers and administrators of Catholic Universities resisted the implementation of this papal document, and in particular its stipulation for a teaching mandate by the local bishop for those teaching theology. All this is indicative of the wide variation in doctrinal orthodoxy and significant resistance to Papal teaching.

Anti-Catholic Prejudice

Although agnostic or atheistic professors do not believe in God, like many writers, they have a fascination with God and religion. These professors seem haunted by the Christian Faith; the Catholic author Flannery O'Connor spoke of the 'Christ-haunted South,'[65] yet we can speak of the Christ-haunted modern world. Thus they always hold Christianity and in particular Catholicism, in the words of Peter Jenkins, as "the last acceptable prejudice." It is now fashionable to ridicule Catholicism.

A renowned physics professor will make a quip about the creation of the world in seven days as if this literal understanding of creation were the commonly accepted understanding by the majority of Christians. It is, however, unlikely that he will refer in the same sentence to George Lemaitre, the Belgium priest who postulated the theory of the Big Bang. A historian or a sociologist may scoff at the

/documents/hf_jp-ii_apc_15081990_ex-corde-ecclesiae_en.html.
[64] Idem, Part II Art 4§4.
[65] "...I think it is safe to say that while the South is hardly Christ-centered, it is most certainly Christ-haunted. The Southerner, who isn't convinced of it, is very much afraid that he may have been formed in the image and likeness of God."
Flannery O'Connor, "Some Aspects of the Grotesque in Southern Fiction" (essay first presented at the Dorothy Lamar Blount Lecture Series at Wesleyan College, Middleton, CT, October 28, 1960), accessed on November 10, 2014.
http://www.en.utexas.edu/amlit/amlitprivate/scans/grotesque.html

Crusades without mentioning the prior attacks on Christian Europe waged by Mohammed and his successors, and without an explanation of the Christian identity of Medieval Europe.
Everyone *seems* to know about religion, especially professors from other subjects without formal studies in theology. It would be just as absurd as a theology professor making outlandish remarks on questions about organic chemistry or nuclear energy, yet this is common fare in the university classrooms.

The assault on religion, however, begins long before in grammar school and high school. A mother writes about her children.

> "Nowadays there is an overt and aggressive, even shameless attempt to remove God totally from the classroom. Years ago, a middle school science teacher of my son asked the class to research their favorite quote by Albert Einstein asking them not to include any of that 'God stuff' in their assignment. While in middle school, one of my daughters shared that they finally had an interesting assembly program. The so-called God Squad, Fr. Hartmann and Rabbi Gelman, came to the school to speak about ethical behavior, not once mentioning God in their presentation that instead focused on the greater good. The following week, an extremely angry editorial appeared in the local newspaper alleging the violation of separation of church and state simply because men of faith had been asked to speak at the school. I prepared a rebuttal to this editorial but it never appeared in the newspaper."[66]

As will be discussed in the chapter on Science and Faith, it is imperative that teachers and students understand that every science has its proper methodology because each science studies reality from different perspectives and by means of different instruments. Without a legitimate respect for each science's method, people will make ridiculous assertions that may seem true but, upon examination, are false and far-fetched.

----

[66] Conversation with Lisa Kende, October 19, 2014. Lisa and her husband Yoel had four children graduate from an Ivy League School.

A Christian who goes to college needs to be prepared for this treatment in class both from a psychological point of view as well as from knowledge of the Faith. As for the first, he needs to expect that it will happen in one of his freshmen classes, and to be aware that a professor who ridicules Christianity will usually not expect a quick and firm reply from a student objecting to the professor's unfairness and unscientific behavior. At the same time, he needs to have sufficient grasp of the basic teachings of Christianity and of Church history with knowledge about the Inquisition, the Crusades and the Galileo Affair. Prior to going off to college, reading *The Faith Explained* and *How the Catholic Church Built Western Civilization* will equip him or her with a ready defense for such a professor.

The encyclical *Fides et Ratio* (Faith and Reason) provides students and professors with a good account of the harmony between faith and reason, as well as of Christianity's defense of the intellect's capacity to know the truth in the face of a climate of widespread skepticism and relativism.[67] In the same encyclical, Pope John Paul II called for a renewal of the profound unity, in theory and practice, between reason and faith found in Patristic and Medieval thought.[68]

This basic knowledge of the faith and preparation for criticism or indifference of religion should be tempered by a desire for study and dialogue with others. A student should avoid seeing an adversary in every professor who says things that are contrary to their religious beliefs, and at the same time they should be able to learn from hearing and understanding the arguments that counter faith or morals. This attitude will enable their intellectual growth as students and foster future careers as leaders.

In addition to defending their religious beliefs, students should learn more about God through university level courses in which they can understand the harmony between reason and faith. Theology is the study of God through reason illumined by the light of faith.

---

[67] St. John Paul II, *Fides et Ratio*[Encyclical Letter on the Relationship Between Faith and Reason], accessed November 10, 2014 at http://www.vatican.va/holy_father/john_paul_ii/encyclicals/documents/hf_jp-ii_enc_15101998_fides-et-ratio_en.html
[68] Idem, nn. 45-46.

As was pointed out earlier, Modern Universities arose from the Medieval Universities that began as educational centers in which the main areas of study were philosophy and theology. Professors and students appreciated the foundational value of these subjects and spoke a common intellectual language. The same should happen in today's universities. In a few words, the reason that theology is important is that God is the most important being that exists; he has created all that exists and ordered it according to his wisdom. To be ignorant about God is to be ignorant about the world, and about mankind.[69]

God is more important than engineering, business or medicine. He is the reason man can study the world and how to solve or remedy mankind's problems. Without theology, students maintain a rudimentary knowledge about the most important subject in their lives. They cannot appreciate the order and relationship between the material and spiritual creation or the moral obligations, which derive from man's created condition. There are many ethical questions that arise in the course of research and work, which require a basic knowledge of ethics and moral theology. This knowledge gives students an explanation of first principles and analysis that goes beyond an insufficient and often mistaken consensus approach method in the analysis of human behavior.

---

[69] As of 2013, there were 227 accredited schools of theology in the US and Canada. Most of the schools have less than 300 students. Out of these schools, 65% are independent, 19% are university affiliated and 16% are college affiliated; 57% are Protestant, 22% are multidenominational and 19% are Roman Catholic. The number of schools offering advanced degrees oriented for research and teaching is 89. The Association of Theological Schools, *Summary of Selected Institutional characteristics, 2013-2014,* accessed on November 10, 2014 from http://www.ats.edu/uploads/resources/institutional-data/annual-data-tables/2013-2014-annual-data-tables.pdf

In the pursuit of happiness, students face personal suffering and consider the suffering of people. They need ideas and arguments to find meaning in their lives, accepting and transcending suffering. Philosophy and theology provide students with the necessary human and supernatural wisdom. Authors such as Plato, St. Augustine, Boethius and St. Thomas Aquinas impart such wisdom and should thus be required study for all students.

Furthermore, the study of theology enables students to have a greater love for God. The more knowledge of God a person has, the more a person is drawn to love of God and the practice of virtue. The converse is true that the less knowledge of God people have, the less they are attracted to God and to a life of virtue. The family and society suffer the more for this.

What is Natural Theology?

Natural theology is the study of what man can know about who God is and how he acts towards creation and man based on the use of reason alone.[70] This study, which is an aspect of philosophy, has been carried out since the time of the first Greek philosophers who sought an explanation for the universe and human existence.

Natural theology does not depend on revelation, the self-communication of God to men through prophets or God himself, as through Jesus Christ. It is, however, a preparation for supernatural theology that teaches man more fully who God is and how he not only creates but also redeems man.

Because natural theology does not depend on Sacred Scripture or a given religion, it can be taught without prejudice to any religion at any university. Although Christian thought has inspired throughout two millennia natural theology, and Catholic authors have written extensively on the subject, this subject is approached in a way that does not require the acceptance of Christian doctrine.

---

[70] For an introduction to Natural Theology see: Angel Luis Gonzalez, *Teología Natural*, EUNSA, 2008; Brian Davies, Introduction to Philosophy of Religion, Oxford University Press, 2004.

A university education requires the study of the full circle of knowledge, at least the main subjects such as philosophy, theology, history, literature, biology, math, physics and art. Among these, theology occupies the highest place because it is the study of God, the foundation for all that exists. Philosophy too studies God and leads to the study of theology. Both of these subjects establish a necessary hierarchy and connection among all the sciences. Alasdair MacIntyre asserts that "one central task of philosophy (...) is to understand both what kind of claims can be justified within each particular science and how these claims relate to each other. Every science is by itself incomplete and partial. But since each is indispensable for our understanding of the whole, none is reducible to any other."[71]

Each science has its place and proper relationship with the others in the circle of knowledge. When one science usurps the place of another, many errors are made. For instance, most professors would object if principles from chemistry were to adjudicate historical judgments, or if findings in physics were to determine ideas in human psychology. Something similar can be said when various sciences attempt to usurp the place of theology, although it is even worse because of the place theology holds in the circle of knowledge: it is its center. When physics or politics seeks to replace theology, violence is done to knowledge. How can telescopes or subatomic particle detectors analyze spiritual realities such as the soul, grace or angels?[72]

Steve Besau, Catholic chaplain of the University of Kansas in Lawrence, Kansas, has been teaching and working with students for many years. He has witnessed the exclusion of God from the university. The university has failed students since it has deprived them of what they most need, the knowledge of God. He writes:

---

[71] Alasdair MacIntyre, *God, philosophy, universities, A Selective History of the Catholic Philosophical Tradition,* New York: Rowman & Littlefield Publishers, Inc, 2009, 146.
[72] Idem, 147. MacIntyre notes that in the 20th century naturalists have pretended to make physics the "fundamental and unifying science," which amounts to an unfulfilled promise.

"The real loss is not faith in God. The real loss is love. Saint John tells us that "God is love" (1 Jn 4:8). When one excludes God, you cannot truly speak about love. Most people on campus, regardless of their beliefs, would consider love to be the most important, or at least one of the most important, aspects of a good life. So if God is not a part of our discussion, then what is love? Without theology, without God, love is simply a chemical reaction, a meme, a psychological reality or just an evolutionary tool to sustain the human race. At best, love is only what you experience when you leave campus and it is primarily an affection or an emotion. When people have a distorted or imperfect understanding of love, what would we expect to see? Loneliness, sadness and emptiness. These are epidemic among university students. When God is excluded, love is excluded."[73]

Every university student should have as a general study requirement a course on natural theology, and universities should look for the best professors to teach such courses. It should find professors who are wise and practice religion or at least show respect for it. In universities with theology departments, courses are offered titled "the problem of God" or even "the God problem." This title indicates the preconceived notions of the professors. God is not a problem to be studied. He is the Being, cause of all beings that we seek to know better. In other times, these courses were titled "On the Existence of God" or "The One God - De Deo Uno."

A militant atheist cannot teach this course. He is inimical to the study of God and, in principle, rejects it. How can he guide others to a sincere study of God and search for truth and wisdom if he is closed to transcendence? But this is precisely what happens in universities that pride themselves for their secularity. Atheist professors teach theology. Does this make any sense? Neither can atheist philosophers and their texts be the main stay of natural theology. To be sure, they are to be studied, but they should be secondary authors whose views and objections need to be examined once students have adequate definitions and foundations in theology. In other words,

---

[73] Conversation with Msgr. Stephen Besau, October 23, 2014.

Hobbes, Rousseau, Spinoza, Nietzsche and Sartre are not reliable or helpful teachers about God.

There is an understandable reluctance to study natural theology given the nature of today's university and the pragmatic approach of students to learning. Business school teaches subjects that lead to tangible results; biology and chemistry measure and experiment. Theology cannot do this. A mistaken scientific view claims that theology therefore is vague and inaccurate. It is mere conjectures and opinions. Both philosophy and theology advance yet their progress is different from empirical sciences because the soul is not subject to measurements as are material objects.

Having considered the need for natural theology, the question must be asked about who or what is the God that is the subject of natural theology.

What do we Know About God?

In simple terms, God is a perfect spiritual being who is the source of all created beings. In the words of St. Thomas Aquinas, he is the *Ipsum Esse Subsistens,* the Being that Stands on his Own. God is not, as some hold, some sort of natural force that permeates the universe. Nor is God a being that is coextensive with creation; in other words, the world is not God's body. He is an absolute and perfect spiritual being. He is not a material being; he is not composed of matter. Things or beings that are composed of matter and spirit are finite beings that have a beginning and an end. Natural theology studies precisely these assertions and gives arguments to show that they are in accord with reason. It should be said right away that Jesus Christ, who is God, assumed or "joined to himself" a full human nature composed of body and soul yet the divinity of Christ is not composed.

Natural theology studies the many proofs adduced over the centuries for the existence of God. These proofs are demonstrations, rather than mathematical proofs, that show the rationality of believing in a personal God who is creator of the universe. There are five classical demonstrations or ways described by Aquinas that build on Aristotle's philosophy of causation and movement. In addition to this, there are many other proofs including St. Augustine's argument from desire and Blessed John Henry Newman's argument from the moral conscience.

This academic study of God has nothing to do with the pagan gods and deities. The only commonality is the desire to explain causality, love, suffering and justice and to find meaning shared by various monotheistic religions with the Greeks' pre-philosophers. There is more to be said about this though. Many people implicitly think of God in terms of a powerful being that is like man only bigger. So much so that people often think: how could God listen to or be concerned with millions of people? Or how could God create the vast universe that is bewildering to view on a clear night? The perplexity here lies with thinking of God from the point of view of our human limitations. Natural theology consists in the rational study of God's attributes: his power, simplicity, knowledge and goodness. Philosophical arguments indicate that there is one uncreated Spiritual Being who is all-powerful, perfectly simple (not composed), all-knowing and all-good, who has created all that we know.

In addition to the study of the being of God and his attributes, natural theology includes the study of natural morality, which is also considered under other subject headings, primarily moral philosophy and natural law. This comprises a large number of relevant topics for man's relationships with other people and life in society. The existence of one God who is good and just is the foundation of a moral life with objective obligations towards people, obligations which can be known through the use of reason. As Dostoyevsky is purported to have said, if God did not exist, anything would be permissible. But God does exist and he has given his creation and creatures objective laws that order their behavior towards their ultimate good.

Finally, Natural theology introduces us to the study of Judaism and Christianity. It stands to reason that God has communicated with the men and women he made and continues to do so through messengers called prophets and, in the fullness of time, through his own Son. Bishop Joseph Butler, an 18th century English theologian, wrote *An Analogy of Religion, Natural and Revealed,* a particularly clear exposition of what natural theology informs us about revealed religion and theology.[74] It is based on the notion of analogy, which is the knowledge of things through other things that bear a likeness with it. Analogy permits us to know spiritual realities by a certain likeness in the material world.

Without contradicting what has been said, Newman points out the limits and even possible excesses of those who write natural theology, especially since, unlike theology proper, natural theology employs the inductive method to study the facts provided by nature. Natural theology cannot tell us about man's Fall, Redemption, Revelation, the Church, etc. By its nature, it tends not to accept miracles since they are considered an interruption or suspension of God's laws. Furthermore, since it focuses exclusively on three attributes of God, power, wisdom and goodness, it ignores other very important ones, such as holiness, justice and mercy. Thus, when it is not studied together with Revelation and subordinate to it, natural theology can become a substitute for the former and lead to pantheism.

Having enumerated some of the main topics of natural theology, there remains to be considered the different influence that natural theology has on various world religions and the order of importance these religions are given on university campuses. Some religions accept the doctrines of natural theology, others do not. Among the major world religions Christianity is the one that fully accepts and promotes natural theology. Some world religions such as Buddhism and Hinduism accept few rational elements in religion; according to these religions, there are many deities. In these religions, reincarnation of beings into other beings is another accepted doctrine that is contrary to an understanding of the person according to natural theology. Islam is a monotheistic religion, which accepts some elements of natural theology, yet discourages or even prohibits rational discourse about God.

Judaism and arguably even more Christianity seek a harmonious relationship between reason and faith. Christian theology is the study of God and morality based on reason enlightened by faith. Christianity should therefore find a privileged place in the university,

---

[74] Joseph Butler, LLD, *The Analogy of Religion, Natural and Revealed to the Constitution and Court of Nature*, London: John Beecroft, 1771.

which has as its very reason for existence the cultivation of reason. It is thus all the more surprising that, rather than favoring Christian theology and the practice of Christianity, many universities privilege Eastern religions. This is not to say that Buddhism or other religions lack elements that are good. In Buddhism there is, for instance, respect for all beings and a peaceful way of life. These elements, and others in various religions, are considered by Christians as seeds of the Word of God or ideas given to man in an original revelation by God.

That initial revelation by God was later completed over time through further revelation that was gradually written down and approved by the Jewish authorities; this resulted in the Jewish Bible, or the Old Testament for the Catholics. After this revelation of God's covenants with the chosen people of Israel there followed a final and definitive revelation through Jesus Christ, who taught with authority, healed the sick and expelled demons. When he revealed God the Father to his people, he was rejected and he suffered death but rose from the dead as he had foretold. His words and deeds and those of his apostles were later written down, and constitute the New Testament. Together, both Testaments, comprising 73 books, form the Bible or Sacred Scriptures. These texts inspired by God have formed all the generations of Christians from the early centuries of Christianity.

The Bible has been a standard textbook for countless generations. It has been the source of wisdom and moral truth for Western civilization. It has formed the way of thinking of countless people to the point where references to it are contained in all of Western literature and art. It has inspired much of the latter and is a key for understanding it. Many great thinkers, even in the 19th century, were brought up reading the Bible. Abraham Lincoln, the 16th President of the United States, who was most likely a deist than a Christian, read and reread the King James Version of the Bible, and quoted and praised it. Until the first half of the 20th century, the Bible provided the accepted and standard moral code of behavior for all Americans. Likewise in England, the Bible and Shakespeare shaped people's education and the way of thinking.

The study of the Bible, its stories, composition and interpretation is a mainstay of the study of theology at colleges and universities. The

Bible, however, can be studied from different perspectives, as a literary work, as a historical work or primarily as salvation history. Depending on the way it is taught - its interpretation - students have a lesser or greater knowledge of God. In many institutions of higher education, the Sacred Scriptures are studied primarily from the point of view of literature and history. They are thus deprived of the spiritual power they have to draw man into a personal relationship with the living God.

Even so, knowledge of the stories and moral teaching contained in the Scriptures gives people understanding about human beings and the correct manner to live in society; it teaches them to live and act wisely and peacefully. A Jewish friend, whose father grew up under communist oppression in Rumania, wrote of his father: "Josef, a lawyer who did not consider himself a 'religious man', once shared with me that his education included full knowledge and examination of the bible as a literary work. Interestingly enough, all who knew him described him as a man of enormous compassion for others (in fact he dedicated the final decades of his life attempting to obtain retribution from the German government for holocaust survivors in Israel)."[75] All college students would greatly benefit from the study of the Bible, especially if the course they study presents religious faith respectfully.

Bringing God Back to the Classrooms

Students are seeking answers for their questions and deepest aspirations. They are not satisfied by materialism despite its initial allure; they are looking for God without knowing it. It is in the university classrooms and halls where they can begin to find him as adults. Bringing God back into the classrooms entails the recovery of a rational discourse about God and man. It requires a better understanding on the part of university and college authorities of the importance of this type of discourse and an openness to its legitimate place in the university.

For their part, students must find professors who are wise and who respect their search for religious truths. They need to discriminate

---

[75] Conversation with Yoel Kende, October 22, 2014.

among the courses offered, aware that the title of the course and the syllabus discloses the professor's attitudes towards natural and revealed religion. For instance, a course at a top liberal arts college titled "Christianity in Scientific Perspective" gives the impression of a course on how to show what is rational and what is not rational about Christianity. Another top school offers undergraduates a course "Christianity in American Cinema." One would expect to have courses on the Old Testament, New Testament and the Church Fathers before wasting time with Hollywood's description of Christianity. Instead of offering substantive courses and seminars on Christianity, the same school offers various seminars in non-Christian religions. Another well-known liberal arts college offers its undergraduates a course titled "Religion and Sexuality." The course description tells prospective students all they should expect to learn about sexual practices according to different religions and acceptance of same-sex marriage. These do not teach about God's natural and supernatural revelation to man, but instead, they deform students' way of thinking. Students need, instead, a serious knowledge about God and his design for man and the world, which can shape their lives and give them true meaning.

Students have always faced, in one way or another, difficulties with religious belief or practice in the university. When John Henry Newman went to study at Oxford in 1817, he was sixteen. Unlike John Adams' father's wish for his son to become a minister, Newman's father wanted his son to become a lawyer. Newman began his studies at Trinity College where he took seriously both the study of classics and the practice of Christian piety. At Trinity, he made his First Communion in the Anglican Church and, the following year, received Confirmation. His piety contrasted with many of his peers who took religion lightly or even in a hypocritical and blasphemous manner, often receiving Communion after a night of drunkenness. At Trinity and later at Oriel College, he encountered teachers who although very intelligent taught a rationalistic theology. In light of this, he sought private classes with Charles Lloyd, a professor of divinity (theology) who emphasized the role of religious tradition and authority in the transmission of the Faith.

Recommended Reading:

Holy Scriptures: Book of Wisdom, Gospel of St. John, Letter to the Romans.

St. Augustine of Hippo, *The Confessions*, trans. Maria Goulding, O.S.B., San Francisco: Ignatius Press, 2012.

William F. Buckley, *God and Man at Yale: the Superstitions of 'Academic Freedom'*, Washington D.C.: Regnery Publishing, 1951.

Joseph Butler, LLD, *The Analogy of Religion, Natural and Revealed to the Constitution and Court of Nature*, London: John Beecroft, 1771.

G.K. Chesterton, *The Dumb Ox*, South Carolina: CreateSpace Independent Publishing Platform, 2012.

Antony Flew, *There is a God, How the World's Most Notorious Atheist Changed His Mind,* HarperOne, 2007.

Peter Kreeft, *Because God is Real: Sixteen Questions, One Answer,* San Francisco: Ignatius Press, 2008.

C. S. Lewis, *Mere Christianity,* Harper, 2001.

Alasdair MacIntyre, *God, philosophy, universities, A Selective History of the Catholic Philosophical Tradition,* New York: Rowman & Littlefield Publishers, Inc., 2009.

Frank Sheed, *Knowing God,* San Francisco: Ignatius Press, 2012.

Thomas E. Woods, *How the Catholic Church Built Western Civilization.* Washington: Regnery History, 2005.

Leo Trese, *The Faith Explained,* 3rd edition, New Rochelle: Scepter Press, 2000.

V. The Classics and Western Culture

In the Western Hemisphere, the name of Classics is reserved for the great thinkers and authors who influenced the formation of the Greek and Roman cultures, and their books were transcribed and preserved for civilization by the monks of the Middle Ages and Muslim scholars.

The Greco-Roman culture shaped the culture of Europe and America and, despite a general ignorance about its historical importance, remains its foundation. After a brief consideration of the meaning of culture, we will look at some elements of the Greek and Roman culture and at some of its great writers and thinkers. This great cultural patrimony has been transmitted to us through the Latin language and literature, the study of which is central to the purpose of a university.

Culture is the characteristic way of living and thinking of a civilization inspired by the religious beliefs of the members of a society. Culture develops over very long periods of time as its own stories are told and retold. The principal elements of a culture are a civilization's language, religious beliefs, art, music, architecture, customs, and laws. The English historian Christopher Dawson wrote: "Religion is the great dynamic force in social life, and the vital changes in civilization are always linked with changes in religious beliefs and ideals."[76] According to Dawson, Europe - and we can add America - owes its cultural unity to Christianity.

Culture is intertwined with language because concepts are expressed through language. The concepts about God, family, work, justice, and so on, give shape to a language and its proper modes of expression. In turn, language acts on the culture by providing the vehicle for conveying concepts and by reinforcing cultural beliefs and practices.

Western culture, the culture of Europe and America, is the result of the transformation of the Greco-Roman culture by Christianity. This process began with the spread of Christianity in the first few

---

[76] Christopher Dawson, *Progress and Religion: An Historical Inquiry* (London: Sheed and Ward, 1929), 234.

centuries after Christ's death and resurrection. The Emperor Constantine issued an edict of toleration of Christianity in the year 311 AD and, soon after that, made Christianity the state religion. In the 4th century laws inspired by Christian doctrine, such as Sunday rest from manual labor allowing for worship, were passed.

Through the course of more than a millennium, from Imperial Rome to the Middle Ages, a Christian culture was developed and consolidated. In the name of "academic freedom", scholars over the last fifty years in the United States have been teaching that all cultures are the same; they claim that cultures have the same weight and importance and that the Christian culture is just one among others. This was already the case at Yale University in 1951 when William F. Buckley, Jr., wrote *God and Man at Yale.* Without any disrespect to people and civilizations, we think that the Christian culture is superior in many respects to other civilizations. Its elevated teaching about God, customs regarding his worship, respect for human beings, especially women and the elderly, notions of law and justice and understanding of the relationship between reason and faith are unparalleled in other cultures.

Pope Benedict XVI addressed the question of the relationship between cultures in his last encyclical letter. There he explains:

> "First, one may observe a *cultural eclecticism* that is often assumed uncritically: cultures are simply placed alongside one another and viewed as substantially equivalent and interchangeable. This easily yields to a relativism that does not serve true intercultural dialogue; on the social plane, cultural relativism has the effect that cultural groups coexist side by side, but remain separate, with no authentic dialogue and therefore with no true integration. Secondly, the opposite danger exists, that of *cultural leveling* and indiscriminate acceptance of types of conduct and life-styles."[77]

[77] Benedict XVI, *Caritas in veritate*[Encyclical Letter on Integral Human Development in Charity and Truth], 26, accessed on November 10, 2014 from http://www.vatican.va/holy_father/benedict_xvi/encyclicals/docum ents/hf_ben-xvi_enc_20090629_caritas-in-veritate_en.html

The Christian culture, with its Jewish origins, drew the best elements from the Greco-Roman culture. Early Christian writers often considered these elements a preparation for the Gospel. Since one of the goals of the cultivation of the mind is knowledge about the culture in which one lives, the study of the Greek and Roman cultures is fundamental for obtaining a university education and for understanding the Christian culture. This study naturally begins with Greek history and literature.

The Influence of Classical Greek Literature

Homer, a blind old man, was a traveling storyteller, perhaps the most famous bard that has ever lived. In the *Iliad,* he tells of the war between Athens and Troy, and in the *Odyssey,* he narrates the adventures of Odysseus, who after the Trojan War bore great difficulties as he tried to return to his kingdom of Ithaca and his faithful wife Queen Penelope - he had made a goddess jealous. The former is a tale of honor and bravery in battle, as well as of the cruelty and destruction of war. Both recount the virtues and vices of men.

Contemplating the beauty of the island of Corfu, Newman wrote in a letter to one of his sisters on January 2, 1833: "It is an overpowering thought to recollect that the place looked precisely the same in the times of Homer and Thucydides, as being stamped with the indelible features of the 'everlasting hills.'" During his travel in the Mediterranean, Newman read from Greek historian Thucydides.

The influence of Homer on Greek culture and literature cannot be underestimated. In a long passage worth quoting in its entirety, Newman describes this influence:

> "The great poet remained unknown for some centuries,— that is, unknown to what we call fame. His verses were cherished by his countrymen, they might be the secret delight of thousands, but they were not collected into a volume, nor viewed as a whole, nor made a subject of criticism. At length an Athenian Prince took upon him the task of gathering together the scattered fragments of a genius which had not aspired to immortality, of reducing them to writing, and of

fitting them to be the text-book of ancient education. Henceforth the vagrant ballad-singer, as he might be thought, was submitted, to his surprise, to a sort of literary canonization, and was invested with the office of forming the young mind of Greece to noble thoughts and bold deeds. To be read in Homer soon became the education of a gentleman; and a rule, recognized in her free age, remained as a tradition even in the times of her degradation."[78]

The Oxford teacher continues explaining the influence Homer had on Greeks, both ordinary men and gifted writers:

"Xenophon introduces to us a youth who knew both *Iliad* and *Odyssey* by heart; Dio witnesses that they were some of the first books put into the hands of boys; and Horace decided that they taught the science of life better than Stoic or Academic. Alexander the Great nourished his imagination by the scenes of the *Iliad*. As time went on, other poets were associated with Homer in the work of education, such as Hesiod and the Tragedians. The majestic lessons concerning duty and religion, justice and providence, which occur in Æschylus and Sophocles, belong to a higher school than that of Homer; and the verses of Euripides, even in his lifetime, were so familiar to Athenian lips and so dear to foreign ears, that, as is reported, the captives of Syracuse gained their freedom at the price of reciting them to their conquerors."[79]

Homer continued to exercise a similar power over the imagination of children and writers for centuries. Newman, himself one of the great English writers of the 19th century, recorded how he first read and copied fragments of the *Iliad* and the *Odyssey* as a schoolchild.

Greece was a mountainous peninsula in the Aegean Sea made up of many small city-states with a common spoken and written language (even though it included various dialects). Athens, the most important of these, situated near a seaport, saw the birth of democracy and schools of philosophy.

---

[78] Newman, "Christianity and Letters," *Idea of a University*, 258.
[79] Ibid, 258-259.

Democracy was born in the city-state of Athens in the 5th century BC. A Golden Age of Athenian history ensued with famous rulers and orators. The art of rhetoric developed; one of the greatest orators was Demosthenes. It was also in this city where the first university began as a loose convergence of philosophers who taught students who traveled there to spend some years learning at their schools. The greatest philosophers were Socrates and his student Plato, and, in turn, Plato's pupil Aristotle. These men have exercised a major influence on philosophy and especially on Christian thought. When Christianity spread to Alexandria, the Christians in that large city soon found Neo-Platonic ideas an excellent means to explain Christian beliefs on God, justice, goodness and life after death. Others schools such as the Epicurean and the Stoics have also had lasting influence.

One of the paradigmatic passages of Plato is found in the Parable or Allegory of the Cave presented in his work *The Republic*.[80] Plato has Socrates describe a group of people who have lived all their lives chained to the wall of a cave, facing a blank wall. They are prevented from turning their heads and can only watch shadows projected on the wall by things passing in front of a fire behind them. The prisoners give names to the shadows but this is the closest they get to know reality. Socrates then explains that a philosopher is like a prisoner who is freed from the cave and comes to understand that the shadows on the wall do not make up reality. The philosopher perceives the true form of reality rather than the mere shadows. He must pursue the study of the Forms or Ideas and the material world of change, and when he has ascended to the highest level and understood "the reality of the beautiful, the just and the good," he must return to the cave and dwell with the prisoners, sharing in their labors. In this analogy, the cave represents the city or state and the philosopher, the good ruler.

The Greek playwrights explored the themes of human love, hatred and other passions; they advanced and discussed political and religious views in their plays. Aeschylus, Sophocles and Euripides were great tragedians of the 5th century BC. Euripides has had a

---

[80] Plato, *Republic*: Book VII trans. Paul Shorey (New Jersey: Princeton University Press, 1980), 514a-520a.

profound influence on drama down to modern times. He represented mythical heroes as ordinary people and demonstrated sympathy for victims, including women.

Roman Literature and Culture

The Roman civilization and culture superseded that of Greece, when the Roman armies defeated the generals who inherited Alexander's Empire. For centuries, Rome's empire grew and prospered by means of its military power. The success of Rome rested on its incorporation of the Greek culture and Rome's practical genius for government, the construction of roads and other public works. The land and sea communication and the Latin language became the means of communicating the new Greco-Roman culture.

Newman describes the incorporation of Greek thought and literature into Rome:

> "When we pass from Greece to Rome, we are met with the common remark, that Rome produced little that was original, but borrowed from Greece. It is true; Terence copied from Menander, Virgil from Homer, Hesiod, and Theocritus; and Cicero professed merely to reproduce the philosophy of Greece. But, granting its truth ever so far, I do but take it as a proof of the sort of instinct which has guided the course of Civilization. The world was to have certain intellectual teachers, and no others; Homer and Aristotle, with the poets and philosophers who circle round them, were to be the schoolmasters of all generations, and therefore the Latins, falling into the law on which the world's education was to be carried on, so added to the classical library as not to reverse or interfere with what had already been determined.[81]"

Latin, the principal language of the Roman Empire, was to be the medium for preserving and propagating the Greco-Roman culture. Newman explained:

> "And there was the more meaning in this arrangement, when it is considered that Greek was to be forgotten during many

---

[81] Newman, "Christianity and Letters," 195.

centuries, and the tradition of intellectual training to be conveyed through Latin; for thus the world was secured against the consequences of a loss which would have changed the character of its civilization. I think it very remarkable, too, how soon the Latin writers became text-books in the boys' schools. Even to this day Shakespeare and Milton are not studied in our course of education; but the poems of Virgil and Horace, as those of Homer and the Greek authors in an earlier age, were in schoolboys' satchels not much more than a hundred years after they were written."[82]

Virgil, (70 -17 BC), one of the greatest Roman poets, painted a picture of the birth of the Roman empire in his *Aeneid*, closely modeled on the *Odyssey*. At the time of Emperor Augustus, Virgil wished to extol the virtues that made Rome great: courage, military power, simplicity, piety. His great epic poem consists of 12 books written in dactylic hexameter, a classical form of meter in poetry. (Each line has six "hex" or feet. In strict dactylic hexameter, each of these feet was a dactyl). Homer's epic poetry had also been written down in this same poetic meter.

The memorable first lines sing of the courage of Aeneas, the legendary founder of Rome:

> "Arma virumque cano, Troiae qui primus ab oris
> Italiam, fato profugus, Laviniaque venit
> litora, multum ille et terris iactatus et alto
> vi superum saevae memorem Iunonis ob iram;
> multa quoque et bello passus, dum conderet urbem,
> inferretque deos Latio, genus unde Latinum,
> Albanique patres, atque altae moenia Romae."[83]

> "Arms, and the man I sing, who, forc'd by fate,
> And haughty Juno's unrelenting hate,

---

[82] Ibid.

[83] Virgil, *Aeneid,* trans John Dryden, (New York: P F Collier & Son, 1909), accessed November 10, 2014.
http://www.perseus.tufts.edu/hopper/text?doc=Perseus%3Atext%3A1999.02.0052%3Abook%3D1%3Acard%3D1

Expell'd and exil'd, left the Trojan shore.
Long labors, both by sea and land, he bore,
And in the doubtful war, before he won
The Latian realm, and built the destin'd town;
His banish'd gods restor'd to rites divine,
And settled sure succession in his line,
From whence the race of Alban fathers come,
And the long glories of majestic Rome."
(John Dryden, translator)

The *Aeneid* recounts the journey of Aeneas, a warrior who flees the sack of Troy to Italy, of his battle with the Etruscan prince Turnus, and the founding of the city of Rome. It opens with the hero carrying his father, Prince Anchises, on his shoulder along with little statues of his gods to escape from Troy. With this opening, the famous epic is putting forth in the first place the idea of the respect due to one's father and religion. The epic poem recounts the Greco-Roman beliefs many centuries before Christ, and at the same time it propagates these beliefs. Virgil's work has had lasting influence on Western literature, notably in Dante's *Divine Comedy*.

Marcus Tullius Cicero (106-43 BC), another exceptional writer born a few decades before Virgil, was a politician, statesman and philosopher. He had an immense influence on prose in Latin and other European languages. He introduced the chief schools of Greek Philosophy to Rome and created Latin philosophical vocabulary with new words such as *humanitas, qualitas, quantitas* and *essentia.*[84] Newman considered Cicero "the greatest master of composition that the world has seen," and tried to pattern his sentence structure and composition on Cicero.[85] In addition to his admiration for Cicero,

---

[84] Elizabeth Rawson, *Cicero: a portrait* (London: Allan Lane, 1975), 303.

[85] Newman described Cicero's use of language thus: "His good sense enabled him to perceive what could be done, and what it was in vain to attempt; and happily his talents answered precisely to the purpose required. He may be compared to a clever landscape-gardener, who gives depth and richness to narrow and confined premises by ingenuity and skill in the disposition of his trees and walks. Terence and Lucretius had cultivated simplicity; Cotta, Brutus,

Newman praised the beauty of composition of the Roman playwrights, Terence and Plautus, and adapted some of their plays, removing indecent content for the schoolchildren of the Oratory School in Birmingham.[86] Every year up to the year of his own death, he directed the students in a performance of a Latin play.

Latin and Transmission of Western Culture

The Holy Scriptures, originally composed in Hebrew and Greek, were translated into Latin in the early Christian centuries. St. Jerome (347-420 AD), a Catholic priest and theologian, began by revising the Latin texts of the Gospels from Greek manuscripts of the New Testament. After completing this work, he spent over three decades as a hermit near Bethlehem translating the Old Testament into Latin from Hebrew texts. The result was the Latin Vulgate Bible, commonly known as the Vulgate. This major achievement provided the West with the text of the Bible used for preaching, teaching and writing theology by countless generations.

---

and Calvus had attempted strength; but Cicero rather made a language than a style; yet not so much by the invention as by the combination of words. Some terms, indeed, his philosophical subjects obliged him to coin; but his great art lies in the application of existing materials, in converting the very disadvantages of the language into beauties, in enriching it with circumlocutions and metaphors, in pruning it of harsh and uncouth expressions, in systematizing the structure of a sentence. This is that copia dicendi which gained Cicero the high testimony of Caesar to his inventive powers, and which, we may add, constitutes him the greatest master of composition that the world has seen." "Personal and Literary Character of Cicero" from the Encyclopaedia Metropolitana of 1824, accessed November 10, 2014 from http://www.newmanreader.org/Works/historical/volume1/cicero/index.html

[86] Ryan McDermott, "John Henry Newman and the Oratory School Latin Plays," *Newman Studies Journal,* 9:2 (2012), 6-12.

[87] St. Augustine of Hippo, *The Confessions*, trans. Maria Goulding, O.S.B. (San Francisco: Ignatius Press, 2012), 3:4, 55-56.

Augustine (354-430 AD) read widely from the Roman authors. One day while reading one of Cicero's works, no longer extant, he experienced a desire for true wisdom. Of this reading, he recounted:

> "Still young and immature, I began in the company of these people to study treatises on eloquence. This was a discipline in which I longed to excel, though my motive was the damnably proud desire to gratify my human vanity. In the customary course of study I had discovered a book by an author called Cicero, whose language is almost universally admired, though not its inner spring. This book of his is called the *Hortensius* and contains an exhortation to philosophy. The book changed my way of feeling and the character of my prayers to you, O Lord, for under its influence my petitions and desires altered. All my hollow hopes suddenly seemed worthless, and with unbelievable intensity my heart burned with longing for the immortality that wisdom seemed to promise. I began to rise up to in order to return to you."[87]

St. Augustine's extensive writing on the Sacred Scriptures and religious subjects has arguably had more influence on Christian thought than any other thinker. Many passages of his works, though translated into modern languages, have, like Cicero's, an expressive beauty and power of expression.

Boethius (480-524 AD) was the last great Roman philosopher, statesman and writer. He wrote his famous *De Consolatione Philosophiae* in prison contemplating an unjust death after a virtuous life. This, his last book, which deserves to be read by every educated person, contains beautiful prose and poetry on the nature of happiness and truth. In *De Consolatione Philosophiae* we find allusions to the Greek and Roman philosophers and poets. Like Augustine's *City of God,* it is one of the works of literature most translated in world literature, which served for the education of many generations even into the 19th century. Boethius was the link between Antiquity and the Middle Ages.

Shortly after Boethius, the Benedictine Monks throughout Europe preserved the classical works, copying the important manuscripts by hand.

"During the short rule of Abbot Desiderius at Monte Cassino, his monks wrote out St. Austin's fifty Homilies, his Letters, his Comment upon the Sermon on the Mount, upon St. Paul and upon Genesis; parts of St. Jerome and St. Ambrose, part of St. Bede, St. Leo's Sermons, the Orations of St. Gregory Nazianzen; the Acts of the Apostles, the Epistles and the Apocalypse; various histories, including that of St. Gregory of Tours, and of Josephus on the Jewish War, Justinian's Institutes, and many ascetic and other works; of the Classics, Cicero de Naturâ Deorum, Terence, Ovid's Fasti, Horace, and Virgil. Maurus Lapi, a Camaldolese, in the 15th fifteenth century, copied a thousand volumes in less than fifty years."[88]

The Medieval universities, rising out of the Cathedral schools, taught the seven Liberal Arts (the *Trivium* and the *Quadrivium*), which had been studied in the universities at Athens and Alexandria. Grammar, the first discipline in the medieval *Trivium*, consisted in the study of Latin composition and the reading from an extensive list of authors. Young monks prepared for copying works from the literary classics and religion by reading the following authors: in Latin from Virgil, Lucan, Statius, Terence, Sallust, Cicero, Horace, Persius and Juvenal, and from Christian poets from Prudentius, Sedulius, Juvencus and Aratus.[89]

Most theologians in the West wrote in Latin. St. Thomas Aquinas (1225-1274), one of the greatest theologians of all time, wrote and dictated his works in a simple Latin unlike the classical Latin of Augustine. Towards the end of his life, he composed two beautiful Eucharistic hymns in Latin, *Adoro te devote* and *Pange Lingua.* Both compositions excel in their theological depth and elegant simplicity. An example of these traits drawn from the *Adoro te devote* is the phrase "Peto quod petivit latro poenitens," where the humble petition to Christ is expressed through the beautiful repetition of consonants called alliteration. Aquinas had the keen intelligence to appreciate the genius of Aristotle and embraced his philosophical

---

[88] John Henry Newman, "The Mission of St. Benedict," *Historical Sketches* (London: Longmans, Green, and Co., 1906) Vol. II, 413. By the name St. Austin is to be understood St. Augustine.
[89] Newman, "The Benedictine Schools," *Historical Sketches*, 460.

realism despite Aristotle's belief in God as an impersonal "unmoved mover." Furthermore, Aquinas made a brilliant synthesis between neo-Platonic, Aristotelian philosophies and Biblical faith.

Dante Alighieri (1265-1321), the great Italian poet, wrote his famous work, the *Divine Comedy*, in the then nascent Italian rather than in Latin. Still, his masterpiece was wedded to the Roman culture, as epitomized in the *Aeneid*. Such was Dante's admiration for Virgil that, in the *Divine Comedy*, he chose him as his guide through the Inferno and Purgatory. Through his poem, Dante transmits to modernity the rich heritage of thought and literature of Antiquity.

Medieval writers and scholars for the most part wrote in Latin, a practice that continued with the humanists of the Renaissance, among whom St. Thomas More and Erasmus of Rotterdam stand out for their accomplishments. These writers, however, returned to the classical Latin composition. In 1516, Erasmus published a new translation of the New Testament, both in Latin and Greek. It was a critical edition or scholarly translation based on the Vulgate Bible and earlier Latin and Greek texts of the New Testament.[90] More taught Latin to his daughter Margaret and, when traveling on business affairs, would correspond with her in Latin instead of English.

After this brief consideration of the classics, can there be any doubt as to their importance in education? The desire to know them arises spontaneously. They contain what is most noble of our Western heritage. To know of them and about them is to know better one's past and to chart the best path for the future. Alexis de Toqueville, author of *Democracy in America,* dedicated two pages of his work to the study of Greek and Latin where he wrote: "Everyone who aspires to excel in literature in a democratic nation should feast often on the works of Antiquity."[91] Their study should be part of every university education, whether in their original language or in a translation.

---

[90] In 1527, a fourth edition of Erasmus' translation of the New Testament contained parallel columns in Greek, Latin and Erasmus' Latin text.

[91] Alexis de Tocqueville, *Democracy in America* (New York: The Library of America, 2004), 546.

Naturally, the classics in their original Greek or Latin are preferable, but reading them requires good proficiency in these languages. When this skill is lacking, the next best option is recourse to good translations.

In the United States, Latin grammar and literature were part of the curriculum of some public secondary schools until the mid-1960's when the enrollment in Latin dropped significantly.[92] Since then it remains an optional subject in private preparatory high schools. Many colleges and universities still offer courses although the number of students enrolled in these is small. Interest and funding for departments in the Classics has decreased. The study of Latin, however, is still possible and depends on the interest of students, which in turn depends on awareness of the importance of Latin for culture, history, science and religion.

History and historical research rely on the study of records or inscriptions on monuments and tombs written in Latin or in other ancient languages with subsequent translations to Latin. Research on Western history, in the period encompassing Imperial Rome until the 18th century, is inconceivable without adequate knowledge of Latin. Scientific terminology in a vast number of fields is based on Greek and Latin words. Some knowledge of these languages facilitates learning necessary basic vocabulary, especially in biology and medicine.

As a language, Latin has many reasons to recommend itself. It trains the mind to think in a logical and orderly manner and to understand English and the Romance languages. Knowledge of Latin helps a student to acquire English vocabulary and improve his sentence

---

[92] In 1948 an estimated 429,000 high school students (7.7 % of all students) studied Latin in public secondary schools in the US. The number dropped to 177,000 (1.3%) in 2000.
U.S. Department of Education, "Enrollment in foreign language courses compared with enrollment in grades 9 through 12 in public secondary schools: Selected years, fall 1948 through fall 2000," *Digest of Education Statistics* (NCES prepared 2002), accessed November 10, 2014.
http://nces.ed.gov/programs/digest/d09/tables/dt09_056.asp

construction and style, especially after exposure to the great Latin writers such as Cicero and Horace. Study of Latin introduces students into the long tradition of the arts where works of art do not stand in a vacuum but build on previous works.

In the West, there has been a great literary conversation for the last three millennia, and to join that conversation, a student needs to have read at least some of the Classics and the Sacred Scriptures. Otherwise, he will not have the necessary points of reference to understand and appreciate the literature of his time or preceding centuries. Shakespeare, for instance, borrows from Chaucer and from a tradition of tragic love dating to Ovid. As we have noted, Dante takes from Virgil who in turn borrows from Homer. At the same time, Cervantes, Shakespeare, Milton, Manzoni, Dickens, Dostoyevsky, Tolstoy, and other great modern authors make little sense without knowledge of the Bible.

For Christians, however, the study of Latin has an even greater significance. Jesus Christ was born in Judea in a Roman Province. When he was crucified, the inscription placed on the cross was in Latin, Greek and Hebrew. Within thirty years of his death and resurrection, the Christian faith had taken root in Rome, the capital of the empire, where Latin was the official language.[93] During the *Pax Romana*, the two centuries of growth of the Roman Empire beginning with Augustus Cesar, Christianity began to spread throughout the Roman Empire, facilitated by good roads, abundant commerce and Christians who enrolled as soldiers in its armies or converted as soldiers.

The liturgy was celebrated in Aramaic, Greek and Latin, depending on the location, but the See of Rome became the head of the Catholic Church; and as Christianity spread far and wide in the Roman

---

[93] I am indebted to Barbara Wyman, instructor of English and Classics at McNeese State University, for her ideas on this subject. She thinks students should be told: "Read Homer because in Homer, you will find Christ. Read Sophocles because in Sophocles you will find Christ. Read Virgil because in Virgil you will find Christ . . . Learn Latin because you will more fully understand the Church -- through which you will more fully understand Christ."

93

Empire, the doctrine of the Church and the writing of its bishops and saints became abundant in Latin. From the 4th century on, Latin became the universal language of the liturgy for the West and gave expression to the depth of the Church's theology and prayers in the Holy Mass and the Liturgy of the Hours. Although, in recent decades, Latin has been unofficially replaced by vernacular languages, it has not been completely eclipsed; and it remains the repository and point of reference for the Church's prayer.

The rich heritage of Latin - for almost two millennia - in the liturgy and theology constitutes in itself more than sufficient reason for studying Latin. Yet, aside from this religious motive, a proper cultivation of the mind calls for the study of both the Classics and Latin. A real university education is seriously incomplete without it. Recognizing this truth, students should find means for studying both, whether in private or at a university. The worthwhile goal of studying Latin can be pursued through other small group settings and special courses in or outside the university.

After this consideration of the role of the Classics and the Latin language in Western culture, we could ask if a liberal education is still possible or desirable today in the United States. The philosopher Mortimer J. Adler (1902-2001) would give a strong affirmative answer. Adler was born in New York City to Jewish immigrants. While working as a copy boy at a newspaper and taking night classes, he discovered the writings of important thinkers who became his heroes. He went on to study at Columbia University and afterwards to teach philosophy at the University of Chicago Law School at the invitation of Robert Hutchins, the newly appointed president. Together they founded the *Great Books of the Western World* program that published, with the Encyclopedia Britannica, a collection of the best books of the Western canon to help people to acquire or improve their liberal education. He also introduced the *Paideia Proposal*, an educational reform plan for the liberal education of children. His lifelong pursuit of the truth and reading of St. Thomas Aquinas since his early twenties led him to be baptized and become Anglican in 1984. Later, after the death of his wife, he was received into the Catholic Church. One of his friends, Professor Ralph McInerny wrote, "he became the Roman Catholic he had been training to be all his life."[94]

Recommended Reading:

Christopher Dawson. *Progress and Religion, An Historical Inquiry.* Sheed and Ward London, 1929.

Homer. *The Iliad of Homer,* trans. Robert Fagles. Penguin Classics, 1998.

Homer. *The Odyssey of Homer,* trans. Robert Fagles. Penguin Classics, 2006.

John Henry Newman. *Historical Sketches, Vol. II.* London: Longmans, Green, and Co., 1906.

John Henry Newman. *Idea of a University.* University of Notre Dame Press, 1982.

The Aeneid of Virgil, trans. by Robert Fagles, Viking Adult, 2006.

---

[94] Ralph McInerny, "Memento Mortimer," found on *The Radical Academy* website, accessed November 10, 2014; *I Alone Have Escaped to Tell You: My life and pastimes* (Louisiana: University of Notre Dame Press, 2006). http://radicalacademy.com/adlerarticlemcinerny2.htm (Radical Academy)

In this chapter we will discuss the place the natural sciences occupy in the university, and ask why a liberal arts education matters for a student majoring in sciences.

We live in a world that for over four hundred years, especially the last one hundred years, has seen remarkable scientific discoveries in the natural sciences and advances in the applied sciences. Theology and the Western Classics seem something of the past with little use or future. Empirical sciences, unlike theology, are progressive and, as such, always advancing and producing results, many of them with practical usefulness.[95] Developments in medicine, such as antibiotics, anesthesia, transplants and regenerative medicine, in transportation, communications and engineering, especially in computation, have effected major changes in people's work, health and entertainment. All this progress and the promise it holds come, however, with important questions often not addressed about the future of man and his relationship to nature, and the very foundations and limits of scientific work and research.

A large percentage of students choose university programs in basic or applied sciences. Contemporary universities have become large research centers engaged in many narrow independent research projects, driven by research grants and involving extensive lab work. Universities, and to a lesser degree colleges, now have a different configuration and ideal: the ideal is no longer the cultivation of the person, body and soul, but the discovery and publication of very

---

[95] Newman held that "Natural Theology, then, is not a progressive science. That knowledge of our origin and of our destiny which we derive from Revelation is indeed of very different clearness, and of very different importance. But neither is Revealed Religion of the nature of a progressive science ... In divinity there cannot be a progress analogous to that which is constantly taking place in pharmacy, geology, and navigation." Newman, "Christianity and the Physical Sciences" in *Idea of a University,* 437. Newman acknowledges that there is development or growth in Catholic doctrine, but this development has different characteristics and pace.

specific and complex findings in molecular biology or physics, or new applications in computer science and other engineering sciences.

Natural Sciences and Applied Sciences in the Modern University

It is common for students in science majors to learn abundant scientific information about a given topic without knowing about other aspects of science or considering the foundations of that very science. Philosophy has lost the role it had of organizing the other disciplines at the university and providing a common foundation for knowledge. The Aristotelian-Thomistic realist philosophy enabled teachers and students to know the whole and the relations of the parts to the whole; to study things not only by their efficient cause but also by their final cause and to give the necessary importance to ethics. Today the training of students is narrow, as is the research, to the point where, within a department of natural sciences and applied sciences, there are few general meetings for all faculty and students. The few vestiges of this are administrative faculty meetings or medical Grand Rounds at teaching hospitals.

The loss of a liberal arts education prior to professional studies in science has had a marked effect on students who lack the wisdom acquired through liberal learning. This lack of an adequate philosophical foundation is evident in the case of the medical science. Medical students enrolled in schools that have courses or seminars in ethics fulfill the requirement but often consider the classes and discussions a waste of time. They would rather know hard facts and avoid ethical considerations, which they think end in sentimental decisions. They have been brought up as undergraduates to think that real knowledge is only scientific knowledge, while the rest is a matter of opinion.

Most of these students, once they become physicians, will not know how to speak with a patient who has to make decisions about treatment with the risk of possible death. They will avoid spending time with a dying patient and speaking with his family. It is not necessarily a lack of good will, but it indicates the incapacity to think and talk about pain, the meaning of suffering and death. That has not been part of their education and training. Everything is tests, numbers and medical procedures or drugs.

The lack of the necessary sensibility and language with which to speak with patients' families is verified in hospital ICU's, where families are often informed by a host of specialists that their relatives are a little better, stable or a little bit worse, depending on various indicators which measure the functioning of the lung, heart, kidney, liver, brain, etc. Often only the nurse will honestly tell the family that the patient as a whole person is really going nowhere or being kept artificially alive with little prospect of significant improvement.[96] Those who still remember the figure of the family doctor or internist rightly ask: What has happened to the time-honored doctor-patient relationship? The answer admits of various explanations; the most fundamental one is that it is next to impossible to be a good physician without a humanistic formation. The liberal arts enable physicians to think of the patient and his family as a whole and to accompany them at the time of illness and death.

History of Natural Sciences

It is worth briefly considering the history of the development of natural sciences to understand how we reached the current state in which the natural sciences stand at the top of the other university disciplines. Although Greek philosophers had speculated on the origin of living things and commented on the Hippocratic medical corpus, Aristotle was the first major natural scientist whose work in human anatomy, physiology, pathology and zoology became the reference point until the 16th century.[97] He made the first systematic and comprehensive study of animals, a study that makes up roughly a quarter of his extant corpus.

His method consisted in a detailed observation of plants and animals, their classification by means of definitions, and an explanation of

---

[96] It is actually illegal for a nurse to tell the patient or family anything the attending physician does not want them to know. Following a chain of command, the nurse has to ask the medical team to be realistic with the patient and family, then ask the attending to do the same before going to the Ethics Committee.

[97] See "Aristotle's Biology" in The Stanford Encyclopedia, http://plato.stanford.edu/entries/aristotle-biology/#AriSciAristotle's Biology

their functions. His physical science was based on a philosophy of science and a philosophy of nature, which identified the essence or form of living things by virtue of the nature of each thing.[98]

Claudius Galen (AD 129 – c. 200/c. 216), better known as Galen of Pergamon, was a renowned Greek physician, surgeon and philosopher whose research and theories had a great influence in Western medical science for 1300 years. He was strongly influenced by the then theory of humors of Hippocratic physicians but he made many anatomical reports. By means of the dissection of monkeys, he added to Aristotle's observations. His theory of circulation endured until William Harvey's publication of the treatise *Motu cordis* in 1648. Galen considered himself a physician and a philosopher, and his use of direct observation, dissection and vivisection was like a middle ground between the rationalists and empiricists of his age.[99]

During the Middle Ages, important historical figures in the development of the natural sciences were Roger Bacon and Nicholas of Cusa. Roger Bacon (c. 1214-1292), an English philosopher and Franciscan friar who taught at Oxford, emphasized the study of nature through empirical methods and is credited as one of the persons who advanced the modern scientific method inspired by Aristotle and later Arabic scholars such as Alhazen.[100] Nicholas of Cusa (1401-1464), combined his work of bishop and papal legate to scientific work, giving great importance to the role of mathematics in

───────────────

[98] In his *Prior and Posterior Analytics* Aristotle explained his manner of proceeding. "The goal of inquiry was a system of concepts and propositions organized hierarchically, ultimately resting on knowledge of the essential natures of the objects of study and certain other necessary first principles. These definitions and principles form the basis of causal explanations of all the other universal truths within the domain of study. Those other universal truths should identify attributes belonging to a subject per se, in virtue of that subject's nature." Ibid.
[99] See "Galen" in Wikipedia. Galen wrote a treatise entitled "That the Best Physician is also a Philosopher," ibid.
[100] See "Roger Bacon" in Wikipedia, http://en.wikipedia.org/wiki/Roger_Bacon

science, improving himself various instruments for scientific measurement.[101]

Francis Bacon (1561-1626), also an Englishman, was a lawyer, Member of Parliament and natural philosopher, who advocated the inductive method in modern sciences. This method goes from particular observations of sensible experience to propositions (or lower axioms) and from these to more general ones. The objective is to reach more fundamental laws of nature, which leads to practical deductions as new experiments or works.[102]

Bacon rejected the old Aristotelian logic and method in science. Rather than examining nature to deduce new theories, Bacon sought to "interpret nature" by means of induction.[103] In his treatise *Novum Organum Scientiarum* (*The Advancement of Learning*), Bacon conceived a vision of science as the triumph of art over nature (*victoria cursus artis super naturam*). According to Pope Benedict XVI, this new correlation between science and praxis or mastery over nature has a theological application: "the restoration of the lost 'Paradise' is no longer expected from faith, but from the newly discovered link between science and praxis. It is not that faith is simply denied; rather, it is displaced onto another level—that of purely private and other-worldly affairs—and at the same time it becomes somehow irrelevant for the world."[104]

This programmatic vision for science was a new *faith in progress.* Francis Bacon and natural scientists, however, continued to hold their belief in a Creator God. For Copernicus, Kepler, Galileo and Newton, who were Christians, the natural sciences did not conflict with the doctrine of creation and providence. Despite the different methods employed by the natural sciences and theology, these two ways of knowledge were not immediately pitted one against the

---

[101] Angel Guerra Sierra, *Hombres de Ciencia, hombres de fe,* Rialp, Madrid, 2011, 132-136.

[102] See "Francis Bacon" in Stanford Encylcopedia of Philosophy, http://plato.stanford.edu/entries/francis-bacon/#SciMetNovOrgTheInd

[103] Idem.

[104] Benedict XVI, Encyclical Letter *Spe salvi,* Vatican Press, 2007, n 17.

other. However, during the late Middle Ages, the separation between the natural sciences and natural philosophy and theology began to increase. For those seeking control over nature, *faith in progress* was considered the result of reason and freedom overcoming the authority of the Church and political structures.[105] This separation grew as the measurement in the natural sciences and description of laws became more and more central to scientific work.

The body of knowledge of natural sciences, especially physics, chemistry, geology, anatomy and physiology, increased greatly in the subsequent centuries. This was made possible through an increase in experimentation. By the 20th century, this scientific method had resulted in such an abundant knowledge of material causes (secondary causes) and had become so prevalent that knowledge was often reduced to scientific knowledge. The final cause of things, sought by philosophy and theology, was put aside as impossible to verify and unimportant. Ultimately, more scientists accept a materialistic philosophy, which reduces all of nature to matter alone and rejects any explanation of final causality and reference to the non-material or spiritual dimension of things. Certainly many scientists do not accept this philosophy but it often underlies the teaching of science in classrooms and popular documentaries on cosmology and earth sciences.

Foundations and Limits of Science

Teachers and students need to ask or, in other cases, reexamine the foundations and method of science. By natural or empirical science, we understand the objective study of material realities by means of quantifiable measurements and tests that can be reproduced. A broader definition of science is the study of a subject by its causes. In the case of the natural sciences, this study is predominantly but not exclusively by means of an inductive method. The results of the empirical sciences are often applied to a wide variety of human needs or activities with notable success.

Mathematics and more recently molecular biology serve as the language of science. This precise language enables man to examine

---

[105] See *Spe Salvi,* n. 18.

the created world and its material causes. It is a beautiful language which Francis Collins, director of the Human Genome Project, referring to DNA, called "the language of God."[106]

The language and method of science defines its limits. Thus, science does not study spiritual beings such as God, angels or humans, inasmuch as the latter are spiritual beings. It cannot adequately study the spiritual soul and its exercise of moral freedom. When scientists reach conclusions outside of their field of study and the scientific method, they incur the error of studying spiritual realities with inadequate instruments. Newman calls physics a "philosophy of matter" which studies the sensible world. It begins with matter and ends with matter:

> "Its basis of operations, what it starts from, what it falls back upon, is the phenomena which meet the senses. Those phenomena it ascertains, catalogues, compares, combines, arranges, and then uses for determining something beyond themselves, viz., the order to which they are subservient, or what we commonly call the laws of nature. It never travels beyond the examination of cause and effect. Its object is to resolve the complexity of phenomena into simple elements and principles; but when it has reached those first elements, principles, and laws, its mission is at an end."[107]

If the physicist is a religious man, he will have definite views on the subject, but that is as a religious man, not as a physicist. As the latter, he has nothing to say and, if he does, he gets himself into "inextricable confusion." A scientist is entitled to voice his knowledge or opinions on religious matters, but when he does he must specify that it is not as physical scientists.

Scientism is precisely the error of claiming that empirical sciences are the only legitimate avenue of knowledge for human beings. It holds that those things that cannot be verified by scientific methods

---

[106] Francis S. Collins, *The Language of God: A Scientist Presents Evidence for Belief,* Free Press, 2006.
[107] Newman, "Christianity and the Physical Sciences" in *Idea of a University,* 432.

are false or uncertain. This error has no other foundation than the assertion of those who hold it. It is an unproven and far-reaching assumption that has been popularized by Carl Sagan, Richard Dawkins and others that ridicule knowledge other than that of experimental science.

Science needs a foundation; it cannot be its own foundation. The study of this foundation is to be found in the philosophy of science and philosophy of nature. The latter asks what is matter, time, light, change, causality, etc. - questions to which the empirical sciences are not capable of giving answers. Although these sciences are always studying these subjects, they do not have good answers to some basic questions about what they are.

Newman asserted that within the limits of phenomena, a scientist can trace the past and anticipate the future and the decay of matter, but he is unable to answer certain fundamental questions:

> "He will not come near the questions, what that ultimate element is, which we call matter, how it came to be, whether it can cease to be, whether it ever was not, whether it will ever come to nought, in what its laws really consist, whether they can cease to be, whether they can be suspended, what causation is, what time is, what the relations of time to cause and effect, and a hundred other questions of a similar character."[108]

Harmony Between Science and Faith

Newman noted that some people claim there is an antagonism between the declaration of religion and the findings of scientific research. This leads to a mutual suspicion between scientists and theologians:

> "The consequence is, on the one side, a certain contempt of Theology; on the other, a disposition to undervalue, to deny, to ridicule, to discourage, and almost to denounce, the labours of the physiological, astronomical, or geological investigator."[109]

---

[108] *Idea of a University*, 433-434.
[109] Idem, 429.

Newman explained that knowledge could be divided into two great circles: natural knowledge that can be ascertained through natural powers and supernatural knowledge that requires God's revelation to man. Although there are points of intersection, these two types of knowledge cannot contradict each other:

> "These two great circles of knowledge, as I have said, intersect; first, as far as supernatural knowledge includes truths and facts of the natural world, and secondly, as far as truths and facts of the natural world are on the other hand data for inferences about the supernatural. Still, following this interference to the full, it will be found, on the whole, that the two worlds and the two kinds of knowledge respectively are separated off from each other; and that, therefore, as being separate, they cannot on the whole contradict each other."[110]

He noted that someone who knows all there is to know about physics, politics and geography will not have the elements to decide the question of whether or not angels exist. Neither will St. Augustine nor St. Thomas, on the basis of dogmatic and mystical knowledge, know more about the motion of the planets or economics than a farm hand. Thus, Newman sustains the impossibility of collision between science and theology. Yet he offers two examples where, in practice, scientists and theologians, overstepping the boundaries of their respective sciences, have collided: the interpretation of Scripture prophecies about the end of the world and cosmology.[111] A third example to which he does not refer in the essay quoted above is the evolution of species. But as far as the third case is concerned Newman did not think Darwin's hypothesis was incompatible with the Christian faith; for him "Darwinian evolution presupposed the existence of a Creator."[112]

---

[110] Idem, 430.

[111] Idem, 443-444. Thomas E. Woods offers a very good account of the often misunderstood and misrepresented case of Galileo Galilei in chapter 5, "The Church and Science" in *How the Catholic Church Built Western Civilization,* Washington: Regnery History, 2005, 66-114.

[112] Ryan Vilbig, "John Henry Newman's View of the "Darwin Theory,"" *Newman Studies Journal,* 8:2 (2011), 52-61.

Rather than fall into antagonism between science and faith and the resulting scientism of Sagan and Dawkins, teachers and students should seek the harmony that exists between science and faith. When the autonomy of each of these fields of knowledge is respected, both are enriched. Whereas science tells of sensible facts, phenomena and results, theology tells us about the Author of nature. The physicist studies the efficient causes; the theologian, the final ones.

In addition to the great medieval physicists who respected knowledge acquired through faith, there have been other notable examples of scientists who did likewise such as Albert the Great, Gregor Mendel and Louis Pasteur. These three great men of science were, like so many others, exemplary Catholics. Albert the Great (1206-1280) was a Dominican philosopher and theologian who also compiled many works on the natural sciences. He used the first translations of Aristotle's biological writings from Arabic into Latin as the basis for his book *De animalibus*, but recognized the importance of experimentation in the natural sciences.[113] Mendel (1822-1884) was an Augustinian monk, who through his outstanding research with peas founded the science of genetics.[114] Pasteur (1822-1895), a Catholic of a profound and simple piety, was a chemist and founder of microbiology whose research with microbes made great contributions in medicine, from vaccination and pasteurization that saved the wine industry to debunking the myth of spontaneous generation; he noted, "… a bit of science distances one from God, but much science nears one to Him."[115]

During the 20th century, the most outstanding physicists have shown respect for religious beliefs. Without lecturing on theological questions, their work in physics led them to comment that the universe is inexplicable without an intelligent being. In *The World As I See It,* Albert Einstein (1879-1955) wrote: "The harmony of natural law…reveals an intelligence of such superiority that, compared with

[113] Angel Guerra Sierra, *Hombres de Ciencia, hombres de fe,* Rialp, Madrid, 2011, 122-125.
[114] Idem, 72-102.
[115] Idem, 168-179; Mark Phillips, *Divine Elements: a God-centered introduction to Chemistry,* Indiana: Abbott Press, 2013, 52.

it, all the systematic thinking and acting of human beings is an utterly insignificant reflection."[116]

Einstein did not hold a belief in a personal God, but nevertheless he recognized the superiority of an infinite intellect and the sublime religious feeling evoked by the thought of this intelligence and the universe:

> "Everyone who is seriously involved in the pursuit of science becomes convinced that a spirit is manifest in the laws of the Universe – a spirit vastly superior to that of man, and one in the face of which we with our modest powers must feel humble. In this way the pursuit of science leads to a religious feeling of a special sort, which is indeed quite different from the religiosity of someone more naive."[117]

Georges Lemaître (1894-1966), a Belgian priest, who postulated what later was called the Big Bang theory, based on Einstein's earlier work, did not extrapolate theological conclusions from his scientific work. Lemaître's conduct is an example of the proper separation between science and faith. At the same time, it is true that his theory gives support to the doctrine of creation of matter, space and time. His theory is not a demonstration of this religious doctrine, a demonstration that cannot derive from natural science, but it makes this doctrine more reasonable to the mind.

Both science and faith have points of intersection because they study the universe and man, although from different angles and with different methods. Both can enrich persons providing them with a better and deeper knowledge of reality. For instance, through science we can know about the abnormal growth of tissue in a patient suffering from an illness and of possible avenues of treatment through the regeneration of tissue; and through faith we can know

---

[116] Albert Einstein, "The World As I See It," *Forum and Century*, vol. 84, 193-194.
[117] Albert Einstein [As quoted in Dukas, Helen and Banesh Hoffman. (1979). Albert Einstein – The Human Side, Princeton University Press.]

about the moral suffering of the patient and his relationship with God and others.

There is one particular way in which empirical sciences today can aid liberal arts. The empirical sciences can serve as a corrective to the *humanities* studied today in colleges and universities because these sciences rely on objective measurements of reality. Since the liberal arts have often developed into the study of the opinions of authors, the empirical sciences oblige the liberal arts to rethink their approach to knowledge and truth.

At the same time, the liberal arts, especially philosophy and theology, can help scientists to have a deeper understanding about the nature (foundations) and purpose of science. Furthermore, they serve as a corrective for applied sciences through the study of right and wrong ends, freedom and responsibility in ethics. Without a good knowledge of ethics and morality, the scientific dominion of ethics easily becomes despotic.

Liberal Arts Courses for Science Majors

Many of those reading this book either wish to study and major in science, or are already presently doing so. Can they study liberal arts while majoring in science? And what bearing would this have on their science careers? Having looked at foundations and limits of the natural sciences, we are better prepared to point to some answers to these questions.

Science majors can study some good liberal arts courses while fulfilling the requirements for their major in science. If they choose good liberal arts courses and teachers, as discussed in an earlier chapter, they will accomplish in good part the end of a university education: the cultivation of the mind and the will. Often this can be accomplished by choosing well from the general education requirements demanded for any major. At some strongly research-oriented universities, this will be more difficult because of the smaller selection of liberal arts courses from which to choose.

Students majoring in science and aspiring to scientific work must resist the reduction of reason and knowledge to the results of the scientific method. Through the study of good courses in liberal arts, they can acquire the indispensable human and intellectual formation to live fruitful and meaningful lives as members of various human communities.

The wisdom of this approach, which fosters a harmony between science and other ways of knowledge, is enshrined in the academic policy of Venezuela's Simón Bolívar University, a university strongly oriented towards the empirical sciences. Students there who wish to major in science must obtain a minor in humanities, and students who wish to major in humanities must obtain a minor in sciences.

Those who fear that the study of liberal arts courses or even a major in liberal arts will hinder their chances of graduate studies in science or delay their career in science, fail to see the importance of a philosophical habit of mind and the enrichment the former provides. The humanities will make them well-rounded persons who are not only able to do science but are able to think about science and its relationship to mankind and the world.

Success in a career in science should not be separated from the happiness that comes from liberal learning and the ethical knowledge acquired by means of it. In sum, a liberal education, whether studying some core courses or completing major in liberal arts, is far from a waste of time, and forms part of the necessary preparation for a good career in science.

The life and work of the physician and scientist Jérôme Lejeune (1926-1994) can serve students and scientists as an inspiration. Lejeune discovered the chromosomal defect in Down Syndrome (Trisomy 21), and spent the latter part of his life looking for possible treatments for children *in utero* affected by this illness as well as fighting for their right to life. As a result of his defense of unborn children with Down's, he was ostracized by the medical community, but he remained firm in his ethical commitment to his patients and the Hippocratic Oath. His Christian faith strengthened him in his scientific and medical career, and helped him to be a very good father to a large family and a loving husband to his wife.[118] He was a

---

[118] See Clara Lejeune Gaymard, *Life Is a Blessing: A Biography of Jerome Lejeune - Geneticist, Doctor, Father*, 2011.

man of faith and a man of science, an example of the correct harmony between science and religion.

Recommended Reading:

John Henry Newman. *The Idea of the University.* South Bend: University of Notre Dame Press, 1982.

Mariano Artigas and Karl Giberson. *Oracles of Science: Celebrity scientists versus God and religion.* Oxford: Oxford University Press, 2006.

Clara Lejeune Gaymard. *Life Is a Blessing: A Biography of Jérôme Lejeune - Geneticist, Doctor, Father.* Philadelphia: National Catholic Bioethics Center, 2011.

Robert J. Spitzer. *New Proofs for the Existence of God.* Grand Rapids: W.B. Eerdmans Publishing Co, 2010.

VII. ADVERSITIES FACED AND CONTRIBUTIONS MADE BY CATHOLICS IN UNIVERSITY LIFE

In this chapter we will consider the spiritual and moral difficulties that young men and women face at modern universities, both secular and Christian, and how they can respond to these difficulties. We will also explain how individual Christians and the Catholic Church contribute to the goals of university life: the cultivation of the mind and the soul.

Contemporary universities had a Catholic origin in the Middle Ages, but most universities today have no religious inspiration - they are secular. The reigning culture is that of secular humanism, not that of the 16th and 17th century Christian humanism. Frequently it is a secular atheism, which is usually anti-Catholic. Therefore, it is natural to ask, "How can Catholic students or professors practice their faith while at a university?" or even more, "Is it even possible to study at a university without relinquishing one's Catholic faith?"

There was a time, even in the not too distant first half of the 20th century, that Catholic colleges and universities were robust places of intellectual life and practice of the Christian faith. At secular universities, students could study liberal arts and various professions without an overt attack on their faith. As noted in earlier chapters, this situation has changed dramatically.

The Crisis of American life is reflected in the crisis of university education, and it is also the result of the state of American institutions of higher education. The Archbishop of Philadelphia, Charles Chaput, writes that the American founders "borrowed heavily from the Roman Republic forms, law, institutions, architecture, and virtues."[119] He explains that, as St. Augustine noted in *The City of God,* "Roman success was built not just on greed, pride and violence; it flowed from the early Roman virtues of piety, austerity, courage, justice and self-mastery."

---

[119] Charles Chaput, "Life in the Late Republic: Catholic Role in America after Virtue" *Catholicism in America: Challenges and Prospects,* ed. Matthew L. Lamb (Florida: Sapientia Press of Ave Maria University, 2012), 91-98, 94.

The culture of our modern universities does not reflect these Roman virtues or their Christian counterpart. Furthermore, it is a culture of narcissism "that seems to foster anxiety, self-absorption, and dependency."[120]

Chaput also notes how the Protestant roots of the United States gave this country many good fruits, such as appreciation for personal opportunity and freedom, respect for the individual, religious liberty and reverence for the law; along with bad ones, including radical individualism, revivalist politics and a Calvinist hunger for material success as proof of salvation.[121]

University life today breeds this culture of narcissism and hunger for material success. A student either accepts this vision or rejects it. All too many end up losing their faith and virginity during their university years. Together with this spiritual and moral fall, they often lose their belief in objective truths and in a natural law that can be known and practiced by all, regardless of religious or ethnic background.

The Spiritual Life of Christian Students

Catholic students who go on to higher education, especially in the Western World, need to be strong Christians to maintain their faith. They must embrace the dogmas and teachings of the Catholic faith and live by them. The only way to remain faithful at a university is for them to live the faith with determination and fortitude, with humility and confidence. Otherwise, they will not withstand the constant attacks and prejudice of those who consider Christianity unreasonable, intolerant and superstitious.

Newman asserted that a Catholic university is not a seminary or a convent; rather it is a place for the study and the cultivation of the intellect in which students must learn to reason and to explain their beliefs with confidence. St. Anselm in the 11th century held that faith seeks understanding (*fides quaerens intellectum*). Faith needs to grow, and the questions that arise in the course of the study of many

---

[120] Idem. 95
[121] Idem. 93

subjects require going deeper into the Church's doctrines, understanding the objections and articulating better responses to them. The study of natural theology considered in Chapter Four gives students a foundation in natural reason for many of their beliefs and permits them to discuss religious beliefs with peers as well as reply to professors, some of whom show marked prejudice against religious beliefs.

A Catholic needs to know the teaching contained in the Catechism of the Catholic Church, which is a complete explanation of the dogmas of faith, the sacraments, Christian life (the commandments) and Christian prayer. In 1992, Pope John Paul II gave the Church a new catechism that contained abundant explanations on these subjects with numerous quotes from the Bible, popes, Church councils, saints and other ecclesiastical writers. Students benefit greatly from meeting once a week with other students to read and discuss a few pages. In successive semesters, they can go through the four sections of the Catechism.

Daily reading of the Sacred Scripture is a foundation for Christian life. Five minutes of reading and meditation of the New Testament gives a student a sure footing in life and shows him or her God's will in the interactions and events of daily life. For some decades, non-denominational Christian groups like the InterVarsity Christian Fellowship and Campus Crusade for Christ have organized Bible studies for students on college campuses. In the last few decades, these Evangelical Christian organizations have seen a significant growth in membership because students seek Christian orthodoxy as well as being part of a group which shares their worldview and offers opportunities for friendship. In more recent years, The Fellowship of Catholic University Students (FOCUS), founded by Curtis Martin, has been doing that in a few dozen campuses in the United States. This group, working with Catholic Student Centers, has had significant success in schools such as the University of Illinois and Benedictine College in Atchison, Kansas, and continues to spread to other colleges and universities.[122]

---

[122] Tim Drake, *Young and Catholic: the Face of Tomorrow's Church* (New Hampshire: Sophia Institute Press, 2004), 45-50. Since the publication of this book, the work of FOCUS has spread to many

In addition, Catholics who take seriously their faith must consult the Church's teaching on various matters and seek a response to contemporary questions. At times, they should ask a priest for reading material for those matters requiring more explanation than that offered in the Catechism. When in the mid-19th century Catholic bishops feared that young Catholics would lose their faith at Oxford, which was then predominantly Anglican and Protestant, Newman explained that although Oxford was dangerous, every place was dangerous; the world is dangerous, and yet "you cannot keep young men under glass cases."[123]

How can this danger be lessened, if not averted? - with good spiritual, moral and doctrinal preparation during high school years. Before going to college, a Christian should develop a habit of prayer that is part of a healthy relationship with God. With this habit, he or she will resist the temptation to put God in second place or, worse, to turn his or her back on Him when faced with the pagan environment of most college campuses; for this is what most colleges and universities are like. They are a reflection of society at large, with the added problem that, at this point in their lives, most students do not have recourse to the positive reinforcement of religious and moral values of their family and the Church.

For those who do not have the habit of prayer going into college, they should acquire it as soon as they start. It is as important - actually more important - than registering for courses or moving into a student dorm. A student can compare daily prayer to other activities like going to the gym to work out. The goal is to be healthy or to train for a sport. A Christian needs to do spiritual exercises; he or she needs to maintain a healthy spiritual life. This consists in some brief moments of prayer when waking up, at some point later in the day and before going to sleep. One dimension of prayer is conversation with God, and there is much to converse about with God: one's concerns and fears, acquaintances and friends, teachers and family. During short times of prayer, for example ten minutes in a quiet

---

other university campuses in the United States.
[123] John Henry Newman, "Letter to Sir Justin Sheil (March 22, 1867)," *Letters and Diaries of John Henry Newman,* ed. Charles Dessain (Edinburgh: Thomas Nelson, 1961), Vol. XXIII, 100-102; 101.

place in the afternoon, God gives peace to one's soul and fills it with light.

A special type of prayer, the primary one that nourishes all other prayer, is adoration of Jesus in the Blessed Sacrament of the Altar. In those times of quiet, God's Presence makes itself felt in the soul. Catholic chaplains can attest to the fact that, after praying to Jesus, many students have found consolation in times of difficulty, and others have discovered God's calling to one or another vocation. Blessed Cardinal Newman employed a motto he adapted from St. Francis de Sales: *cor ad cor loquitur*, heart speaks to heart. This saying refers to the communication between close friends; it is having a heart-to-heart conversation. With even more reason, this can be said of Jesus who dwells in the soul of his friends.

J. R. R. Tolkien pointed to this type of relationship in a letter to a nephew:

> "Out of the darkness of my life, so much frustrated, I put before you the one great thing to love on earth: the Blessed Sacrament... There you will find romance, glory, honour, fidelity, and the true way of all your loves on earth, and more than that: Death: by the divine paradox, that which ends life, and demands the surrender of all, and yet by the taste (or foretaste) of which alone can what you seek in your earthly relationships (love, faithfulness, joy) be maintained, or take on that complexion of reality, of eternal endurance, which every man's heart desires."[124]

Through the sacraments, God makes himself present to us and enables us to live as his children. Besides Baptism which is the door to Christian life, and Confirmation which brings an increase and deepening of baptismal grace, the Sacraments of Reconciliation and of the Holy Eucharist are fundamental for the life of grace. Many colleges have a Catholic chapel on campus or a nearby Catholic church where students can easily receive these sacraments with

---

[124] J.R.R. Tolkien, *The Letters of J.R.R. Tolkien*, ed Humphrey Carpenter and Christopher Tolkien (Boston: Houghton Mifflin, 1981), Letter n. 250.

their friends and other persons who make up the Catholic community of believers.

A strong piety informs a person's moral choices and way of life. Students who pray every day more easily stay focused on their studies and make good use of their time. They realize that time is a treasure to be used wisely, the same with the intellectual talents received. A Christian is counter-cultural. In university campuses, this requires a constant effort and the help of like-minded peers. Today's prevalent university culture is characterized by heavy drinking, the use of drugs and participating in "recreational" sex. New students are introduced to this pagan lifestyle as soon as they arrive at college. At the student orientations, they are indoctrinated on the supposed normality of casual sexual relations ("hook up" culture) as well as homosexual and bisexual relationships. In many colleges, they are exposed to the absurd and harmful living situation of co-ed dorms. There are numerous consequences to this decadent behavior such as the loss of faith, depression, sexually transmitted diseases and unwanted pregnancies resolved in abortions. From the first week on campus, men and women must be "rebels," fighting against this pagan culture. They have to insist on living in single-sex dorms and strive to live healthy and meaningful lives.

Without the grace of the sacraments, it is very difficult to resist the moral decadence of college life. The sacraments strengthen us against such temptations and sustain us in our work and relationships with others. Students who attend Mass on Sunday and go to Sacramental Confession regularly, at least once a month, are usually in good spiritual shape and live healthy lives. They are able to promote in their surroundings a good human and spiritual climate and to help their friends to also live upright and spiritual lives. Many students on college campuses have been helped by the example of their friends receiving the sacraments and taking them to Sunday Mass or to Confession. A good Catholic campus ministry has one or more priests who are available every day to celebrate the sacraments and eager to offer students counsel and encouragement.

Catholic Student Centers on Campus

At the end of the 19th century, some Catholic chaplaincies or student centers at secular universities began to adopt the name "Newman Center," after Cardinal Newman. One of the first was at the University of Pennsylvania. Many students find in these centers the grace of the sacraments and the warmth of a community of fellow Catholics. It is not uncommon to hear graduates say that it was because of the Newman Center that they were able to keep or practice their faith better in the difficult university environment. Others discovered the Church through these centers and, after instruction, were baptized or received in the Catholic Church. A good Catholic Student Center or Newman Center is paramount for the healthy spiritual and moral life of students; such a center serves as one criterion for choosing between schools.

Catholic Student Centers that teach orthodox doctrine and promote practices of piety such as Eucharistic adoration and prayer of the rosary have seen a markedly increased student participation in recent decades. This has been the case, for example, at the Newman Centers at the University of Illinois at Chicago and the University of Illinois at Champaign, as well as the Catholic centers at the University of Maryland at College Park[125] and Texas A & M.

Learning has a lot to do with the exercise of piety and virtue. Both facilitate and foster learning in various ways. They bring an inner order and peace to the mind by allowing it to grasp reality and to interconnect ideas more readily. They create an exterior order that favors good study habits, such as waking up at a regular time and dedicating set hours to study without giving in to procrastination or unnecessary distractions. Dedication, perseverance, honesty and patience are some of the virtues that are most important for study.

As mentioned earlier, some thought that useful knowledge and more libraries alone would inevitably bring peace and progress for society. Today, despite the failure to produce the promised results by means

---

[125] Colleen Carroll, *The New Faithful, Why Young Adults are Embracing Christian Orthodoxy* (Chicago: Loyola Press, 2002), 155-197; 183. Something similar continues to happen a decade later.

116

of an exponential increase in the number of colleges and libraries, many still think the problems of the world will be solved with more knowledge and more laptop computers. Liberal education can produce a gentleman and a professional, but they do not make the Christian. It is the practice of human and supernatural virtues that forges character and brings about true peace and progress among men. A Catholic strives to exercise fairness, respect towards people and a genuine spirit of tolerance for others and their work.

Just as important as these virtues is the passion to know the truth and to follow it wherever it may lead. This passion requires an intellectual honesty that is connatural to a practicing Christian. When a person is not enslaved to sensual pleasures or intellectual pride, he or she will more readily and easily reach truths - whether religious, historical or ethical. On the contrary, a person who does not live chastely will end up denying the Church's teaching on marriage and procreation. Someone who out of pride does not wish to be singled out in the history department will accept generalizations about wrongful actions of Catholic leaders in the course of history.

A Catholic holds certain basic and foundational beliefs concerning the dignity of each human being from the moment of conception, the sanctity of marriage between a man and a woman, work as a participation in God's creation, etc. These beliefs and the corresponding moral obligations create a moral ethos that is binding for all members of society and that is the source of peace and justice. While Catholics respect those who disagree with these convictions, they are compelled by faith to articulate and defend them at the university.

So far, we have seen how a Catholic finds many challenges and temptations to practicing his faith in college. On the other hand, a Catholic has the possibility and the mission to be a force for the good. The light of faith gives him or her better understanding of reality than that of non-Christian students and teachers. The intellectual tradition of the Catholic Church and the accumulated wisdom of Catholic thinkers give him or her high ground on which to stand. It is not a matter of acting towards one's peers in a conceited manner but of confidently explaining many truths to them. However, widespread prejudice against believers, Catholics in particular, can put students in a defensive position or an attitude of inferiority.

What are some areas of university disciplines on which the Catholic faith sheds light? Through class discussions, term papers and seminars, a well-formed Catholic can present valuable ideas to his or her peers, for example, on the dignity of the person in the sciences, the existence of objective truth or the nature of man in philosophy, honesty and the common good in business, the existence of natural law in the study of law, and a spirit of service in medicine. In these subjects and many more, Catholics have articulated first principles and established meaningful practices. Over time, these have been accepted by many and are no longer recognized as Catholic, yet they still require a defense, which rests not only on natural law accessible to all but to the arguments presented by Christians.

The Catholic faith challenges young men and women to "refuse to build their own private little worlds"[126] living in a selfish bubble that begins in high school and is enshrined in college. St. Josemaría Escrivá, who established the University of Navarre in Spain and inspired the foundation of close to a dozen other universities, said in an interview:

> "A university must educate its students to have a sense of service to society, promoting the common good with their professional work and their activity. University people should be responsible citizens with a healthy concern for the problems of other people and a generous spirit, which brings them to face these problems and to resolve them in the best possible way. It is the task of universities to foster these attitudes in their students."[127]

The model of most colleges and universities is one that encourages personal advancement through study and research. Service to other members of society is considered something optional to which lip service is paid. The Catholic vision of rendering glory to God through

---

[126] St. Josemaría Escrivá, "The University at the Service of Contemporary Society," *Conversations with Msgr. Escrivá* (California: Ecclesia Press, 1972), 91.
[127] Idem, 90.

one's work and of social responsibility is very different. St. Josemaría explains: "A university should not form men who will egoistically consume the benefits they have achieved through their studies. Rather it should prepare students for a life of generous help of their neighbor, of Christian charity."[128]

Such future service to society, especially to those who lack basic assistance, cannot be postponed for years after college. Respect for the sick, the poor and the uneducated, begins with concern and acts of service for them in the prime of youth. The summer months or Christmas holidays are a good time to engage in various service projects. This service requires generosity, sometimes sacrificing other plans such as vacations, work opportunities or internships. Yet it is through these service opportunities that empathy for those who suffer is promoted and a greater sense of people's need for human warmth and compassion is cultivated. It is in these times that young people discover horizons of lifetime service through future work.

With regard to the nature of learning itself, Catholics bring to the university a vigorous pursuit of truth which is innate in all human beings but which is reinforced by confidence in the order and intelligibility that the Creator has given to the world and a noncyclical view of time. As Fr. Stanley Jaki, OSB, explained, this way of thinking among medieval scholars provided the necessary matrix for the development and consistent growth of science, whereas the ancient Greeks, Egyptians and Chinese did not go beyond some, albeit important, scientific discoveries.[129] The Catholic belief that objective truths exist - that biological processes and cosmic events are regular and not the result of chance or the whims of the gods – and that the development of the scientific method, greatly favored the pursuit of new knowledge.

Various Catholic university centers have given rise to institutes that promote a Catholic intellectual life on campus. One such institute is the Humanitas Institute at the St. Lawrence Catholic Center of the

---

[128] Idem, 91.
[129] Paul Haffner, "Pitfalls and Prospects of Science," *Creation and Scientific Creativity, A Study in the Thought of J. L. Jaki* (Virginia: Christendom Press, 1991), 33-48.

University of Kansas. It offers freshmen and sophomores a two-year program on the best of the Catholic liberal arts education. The Lumen Christi Institute provides students at the University of Chicago with lectures on the Intellectual Catholic Tradition. Other institutes that advance the study of natural law, liberal arts, and faith and reason have opened in various universities throughout the country. The Witherspoon Institute is an independent research center located in Princeton that seeks greater understanding of the moral foundations of free and democratic societies. The Berkeley Institute located at the University of California in Berkeley is another independent community for students and scholars committed to intellectual and academic inquiry rooted in the Judeo-Christian tradition.

Centers like these serve to strengthen the intellectual life of Christians who very often find their college courses marked by skepticism and anti-Christian attacks. At these centers, students find the right climate for intellectual growth - the purpose of a university - within an atmosphere which fosters a healthy relationship between faith and reason. They find a community of students and scholars who wish to pursue intellectual and moral truths with seriousness and respect for their religious beliefs.

Furthermore, beyond natural truths Catholics seek religious truths and answers to man's deepest questions about the meaning of life and suffering. These questions are studied in natural theology, as discussed in an earlier chapter, but above all they are discussed in informal conversations with friends and teachers during the formative years of college. When students share a room or study in the same faculty, there are many occasions for deep conversations on personal matters and lasting friendships often develop.

A Community of Friends

College years are thus years for sharing friendships of varying degrees with a number of people, and gaining lasting friendships. This reminds us of what St. Augustine of Hippo did in Milan shortly before and after his conversion, and later near Hippo in Northern Africa - he formed a community of friends who prayed and studied together. They shared an intense and intellectual friendship, inspiring one another in the study of the classics, acts of prayer and the practice of virtue. This is far from the ambiance of most college dorms where students blast music, play video games until early hours of the morning and waste time on a host of other things. Rather than a *dorm,* the ideal of a college hall with an intellectual and religious purpose should be sought by students and fostered by universities.

From his studies at Trinity College and his teaching at Oriel College in Oxford, Newman appreciated the rich exchange that takes place between friends and peers. As an undergraduate at Trinity, various accomplished men suggested books to him that corrected errors in his judgment about people or the content of his early sermons. He would always remember the kindness of his tutor and math teacher, Mr. Thomas Short, and the confidence he showed in him. It was he who encouraged young Newman to take an exam that gained him a scholarship at Oriel.

When Newman established the Catholic University of Ireland, he drew up plans for small university halls. The idea behind this was to recreate on a smaller scale the Oxford colleges with the formative element of close interaction with peers and the help of a junior Tutor. He emphasized the need for students to exercise their freedom and responsibility and at the same time have the guidance and supervision of older persons. Today's dorms and resident assistants (RA's) are a poor substitute for what Newman envisioned. Newman had in mind a residential scheme for the university, that is, a university made up of residential colleges. Each residence or college would hold twenty students and have a governing body with a dean, one or two lecturers and tutors who lived in the college. It would also have two or three scholars, graduate students on scholarships, who would serve as a medium between the governing body and the students.[130]

---

[130] Newman, "John Henry Newman to Archbishop Cullen," *Letters and Diaries of John Henry Newman* Vol. XV, ed. Stephen Dessain (Oxford: Clarendon Press, 1964), 145-149; Joseph M. Horton, "John Henry Newman's Vision of the Residential College: the Place of Formation in the Process of Education," *Newman Studies Journal,* 9:1 (2012): 44-51.

A good university education is incomplete without a mentor, a guide, to lead a student through the complicated myriad options and obstacles. A mentor is usually a professor, someone with a lot of knowledge and of mature character, who both inspires and challenges his charges. Newman thought that a professor, acting as a tutor "on a smaller number at a time, and by a catechetical method, will be able to exert those personal influences, which are of the highest importance in formation and tone of character among the set of students, as well as to provide that the student shall actually prepare the subject for himself, and not be a mere listener at a lecture."[131] That is what Newman was to a few dozen men who studied under him over the years that he was a tutor at Oriel College.[132] He saw the role of a mentor as a spiritual, moral and academic guide, not only the latter as had become the case in the mid 19th century at Oxford. Newman argued that "[a]n academical system without the personal influence of teachers upon pupils, is an arctic winter; it will create an ice-bound, petrified, cast-iron University and nothing else."[133] College years are too precious, and the energy of youth and variability of emotions is such that each student needs a good guide. This is as difficult to find now as it was during Newman's time at Oxford. Still, it is an important goal worth pursuing with the help of Newman Centers on campus or study centers that the Prelature of Opus Dei has in a number of cities. In practice, it often means finding two mentors, one for academic matters and another for the religious and spiritual.

The following are some practical questions about mentors worth answering briefly: How to find a mentor? How often to meet with him? and What to expect from the meetings? A mentor should be a teacher one admires or one who is well recommended for his

---

[131] John Henry Newman, 'Report on the Organization of the Catholic University of Ireland,' October 1851, *My Campaign in Ireland*, 84-85. Cited by Paul Shrimpton, *The 'Making of Men,'* 64.

[132] Newman was loved by his students with whom he read, walked, and had breakfast or dinner. According to Thomas Mozley, his future brother-in-law, he could be likened to 'a father, or an elder and affectionate brother.' See Paul Shrimpton, *The 'Making of Men,'* 18.

[133] Newman, *Historical Sketches,* Vol. 3, 74.

knowledge and good character. One may know him from a course or lectures one has attended or from reading some of his papers. It is better to wait for a while to find a good mentor rather than rush into this type of relationship. At a given moment, after deciding on who would be a good mentor, one simply has to ask the person if he or she will be one's mentor. Usually a student meets with a mentor weekly or a few times a month for a set amount of time, for example thirty minutes. A mentor is more than an advisor, and the meetings with him are more than "going to a professor's office hours." There are external similarities between a mentor and an advisor but the relationship of student to mentor is a more personal and demanding one than that with an advisor or teacher assistant (TA). In the former, goals are set, difficulties of a personal nature are discussed and far-reaching horizons are opened.

According to John Henry Newman, a university is much more than a formal institution that teaches a wide range of courses and imparts degrees; it is a mother who takes interest and care of each individual member. He wrote, "A University is, according to the usual designation, an Alma Mater, knowing her children one by one, not a foundry, or a mint, or a treadmill."[134] The education that professors, mentors and peers provide is personalized. It helps each person to develop his or her intellectual gifts and other talents, and to grow in the moral virtues.

Furthermore, a good university is one which encourages an intellectual, moral and religious spirit reflected also in its architecture and meeting spaces, as well as in its traditions. Newman wrote: "It is scarcely too much to say that one-half of the education which young people receive is derived from the tradition of the place of education. The *genius loci*, if I may so speak, is the instructor most readily admitted and most affectionately remembered. The authorities cannot directly create it; still they can encourage, and foster, and influence it."[135]

---

[134] Newman, "Discourse 6: Knowledge viewed in Relation to Learning," *Idea of a University*, 144-145.
[135] John Henry Newman, *My Campaign in Ireland, Part I: Catholic University Reports and Other Papers.* Aberdeen: A. King, 1896.

When a student experiences the personal attention of mentor, meaningful college friendships and the *genius loci* of a school, he will naturally look back to his school as his *Alma Mater* (dear mother). The name and thought of his college or university will be associated with pleasant memories of friends and lessons learned as well as the discovery of paths taken in life. The thoughts of its professors, halls, common gathering areas and sports teams will also remain close to his heart. These associations will evoke gratitude and, to the extent that these sentiments exist, there will be a desire to help the school's needs and growth.

The difficulties of maturing and finding one's way in life are not new. There was, however, a time when Catholic colleges and universities provided students with a Catholic *ethos* and milieu that inspired piety and virtue, despite the human frailties of both students and professors. The reality today is that the majority of colleges and universities are secular in the pejorative sense of the word. They not only do not provide this environment, they indirectly oppose it by hiring professors who boast of their atheism, running politically correct study programs and endorsing decadent student activities. Thus, it is up to students to seek or create for themselves a community of friends, which will share their Christian vision of life and foster it. In the pursuit of this goal, Catholic chaplains and lay staff play a very significant role by providing students at Catholic student centers with the human and spiritual environment, which they need to mature and flourish in their faith and university studies.

Recommended Reading:

Aristotle. *Nichomachean Ethics, 2nd ed.* Cambridge: Hackett Publishing Company Inc., 1999 (in particular Bk VIII on Friendship). Colleen Carroll. *The New Faithful, Why Young Adults are Embracing Christian Orthodoxy.* Illinois: Loyola Press, 2002. (chapter: "Campus," 155-197.)

Paul Shrimpton. *A Catholic Eton? Newman's Oratory School.* Leominster, UK: Gracewing, 2005.

Juan R. Vélez. *Passion for Truth, The Life of John Henry Newman.* Charlotte: TAN, 2012. (chapters: "Tutor at Oriel," 121-129; "Debate on How to Make Men Moral, 348-360; "Founder of the Catholic University of Ireland," 528-536.)

VIII. WHAT FOLLOWS COLLEGE AND A LIBERAL ARTS DEGREE?

Many students and their parents who read this may agree with the content of the chapters that precede this one, but all along they have been asking, "What work can be pursued with a liberal arts degree after college?" and more importantly, "How can someone pay student loans and earn a living with a liberal arts degree?"

Simply stated, our thesis is as follows: College undergraduate studies are for the cultivation of the mind and the will through the liberal arts. Graduate university studies are for professional or specialized career training. College study is a period of time to develop a philosophical habit of mind, including learning skills and a broad knowledge in philosophy, theology, history and literature.[136] This gives students the education required to become good citizens, parents and members of a religious body.

When such education is forfeited or reduced to a few general requirements that are fulfilled just to get them out of the way, we then have the proverbial cart before the horse, with students specializing in fields of knowledge without the necessary intellectual and human formation. In other words, many students wish to specialize without having a good intellectual preparation. In many countries, and in recent decades also in the United States, they go to college to obtain a degree in some profession rather than to seek the cultivation of the mind. It is typical for students in Europe and South America to enter careers in medicine, dentistry and law directly from high school.[137] Although the latter does not happen in the United

---

[136] Although Newman sustained this notion on the primary function of a college education he did not confine his curriculum to the classics-based curriculum at Oxford. He envisioned the arts faculty at the Catholic University of Ireland would be subdivided into a division of letters and a one of sciences. The latter would include physical, biological and social sciences, mathematics and a school of engineering. See Paul Shrimpton, *The 'Making of Men,'* 60.

[137] Even though in most countries of South America, Africa and Asia the majority of students and families cannot afford to spend a few years studying liberal arts before obtaining professional training, those students need some courses in the humanities to better

States because a college degree is required, students who plan to study medicine or dentistry focus almost immediately on a major that will prepare them for this.

As was discussed earlier, there are some ways to reduce the costs of a college education - primarily by obtaining scholarships, working during the summer and studying the first two years at a community college. It is important not to accrue a big debt from college and to begin to pay it off soon in order to be able to pursue professional training and various vocations in life such as marriage, priesthood or religious life.

Naturally, after a liberal arts degree, college graduates have to find gainful employment, a job that will pay his or her debts and living expenses. A person who has trained his or her mind well can find employment in many fields, such as teaching, research in various types of institutes, a wide range of sales and management opportunities, university administration and government offices. His capacity for critical thinking, creative expression and work habits enable him easily to develop specific skills needed in the employment he chooses, or to start his own business.

In the *Idea of a University,* Newman compared a liberal arts education to health, which precedes any type of work. He wrote:

> "[S]o in like manner general culture of mind is the best aid to professional and scientific study, and educated men can do what illiterate cannot; and the man who has learned to think and to reason and to compare and to discriminate and to analyze, who has refined his taste, and formed his judgment, and sharpened his mental vision, will not indeed at once be a lawyer, or a pleader, or an orator, or a statesman, or a physician, or a good landlord, or a man of business, or a soldier, or an engineer, or a chemist, or a geologist, or an antiquarian, but he will be placed in that state of intellect in which he can take up any one of the sciences or callings I have referred to, or any other for which he has a taste or special talent, with an ease, a grace, a versatility, and a success, to

understand others, themselves and their place in society.

which another is a stranger. In this sense then, and as yet I have said but a very few words on a large subject, mental culture is emphatically *useful.*"[138]

In addition to a more developed capacity to reason, compare, and discriminate, persons with a broad educational background can understand others more easily and work with them in professional settings. A highly recognized business school in Spain prefers applicants who come with a liberal arts education precisely because of the habits of mind they have.

Having obtained a good undergraduate liberal arts education, students are well positioned to enter into research or professional education. Although liberal arts students can obtain employment, they will often wish to continue their education and will have better remuneration in research or in some other professional field. Indeed, given the realities of the job market, a student who is entirely focused on the liberal arts during their undergraduate years, may want to plan on some sort of specialization. Students who have studied liberal arts as undergraduates often quickly catch up and surpass those who have been trained in specific areas as undergraduates. The decisions to continue with graduate school or professional schools must, however, be well thought out and planned, and thus students in the course of their undergraduate education should begin to take a longer-term perspective on the questions of whether they plan to continue their education into graduate studies, pursue stable work or work and return to school at a later date.

Graduate Studies

Upon graduating from college, many students feel they must continue with graduate studies, since they consider that a liberal arts degree does not give them work opportunities or offer an advantage over other applicants in the work force. Unless, as will be discussed,

---

[138] Newman, "Discourse 7: Knowledge and Professional Skill," *Idea of a University,* 165-166; Jane Rupert, *John Henry Newman on the Nature of the Mind: Reason in Religion, Science, the Humanities* (New York: Lexington Books, 2011).

a graduate has a very clear career plan and financial possibilities to pursue it immediately after graduation, he or she should look for an honest paying job that provides a service to clients and allows for gainful employment and personal development. It is important to resist the temptation to gain a lot of money soon and have the capacity of spending a lot, so often exemplified by friends or characters in movies.

Steady and constant work as well as frugality and living within one's means enable graduates to pay off their loans and marry or work towards other goals. Yet, instead of saving to repay their college debts, college graduates often travel to weddings of friends all over the country, travel to sports events or engage in other expensive activities that are beyond their reasonable means and thus delay their repayment of student loans. They also forget that tried and true path of gradual professional advancement through consistent and reliable work over the course of many years. Additionally, in exchange for a higher salary, a graduate may choose a position with a company that offers to reimburse good employees for advanced degrees. Careful planning is the secret to the successful attainment of one's goals.

Academic disciplines at colleges and universities are divided into three domains: social sciences, natural sciences and humanities. Here we will briefly discuss some of the graduate and professional career paths open to college graduates, considering first the path of graduate studies.[139]

Obtaining graduate degrees is for many people a default path. Once they finish college, unless they can think of a rewarding job open to them, they start applying for master's or even doctoral degrees. As in the pursuit of university studies, students need deliberately to ask themselves: Why do I wish to go on to graduate studies or professional schools? What is the deepest motivation and is it correct? Otherwise, they are drifting without direction and will often

---

[139] In *The Closing of the American Mind,* Allan Bloom offers a critical analysis of the disarray of these disciplines in the contemporary university and a challenge to future generations. Bloom, "The Student and the University," 336-382.

be unhappy in life, going from one academic program to another and one postdoctorate position to another.

College graduates who wish to go on to graduate studies should work for at least a year or two in some employment. While they repay student debts and save money, perhaps living at home, they must carry out a very important task, that of thinking of their future and asking for advice. It should be a period to identify further their talents, skills and dreams, considering how these would best be put to use in society. Equally important is for the graduate to consider the significant social and financial circumstances of the times in which they live. All these factors have a bearing on a decision to pursue graduate studies and particularly which one.

In a similar way that a good sportsperson needs a competent and committed coach, an aspiring graduate student needs an accomplished mentor. The example of this professor or professional will inspire a student. An experienced mentor will serve as a valuable guide to avoid and overcome the difficulties of academic life. During this period of work prior to graduate studies, college graduates should continue with independent reading and study under the guidance of a mentor. The same guide will help a student choose a graduate program with outstanding professors, and possibly provide the needed recommendation.

College students and graduates need an accurate picture of academic programs and degrees. They need to weigh the expense, years of study and long-term career opportunities available to them. In English, languages, history, philosophy and psychology, most graduates in master's and doctoral degrees would naturally look for teaching positions. Besides the anecdotal stories of taxicab drivers with doctorates in English, though I have never met one, prospective students need information about regional employment trends and work possibilities.

Students who have an aptitude for these fields and wish to pursue them should also consider future work opportunities in teaching that are not limited to the top universities; these include the whole gamut of colleges and high schools. In addition, persons with passion and knowledge for given subjects can pursue employment in writing, journalism and various media where their gifts can make a good contribution to society.

Professional Schools

Let us consider various professional schools as career paths for graduates in liberal arts. Graduates with this degree are suited in many ways for these schools even though at first hand they may think they are not and that they will face difficult entrance exams.

Medical School continues to be an attractive profession despite the many changes it has undergone in the 20th century, both in the dramatic increase in medical knowledge, technology and treatment as well as in the deterioration of the patient-physician relationship. The medical profession needs intellectually well-formed men and women who appreciate and respect the spiritual nature of man. Too often applicants for medical school know a lot about biology and chemistry and little about the human person and the soul. Their knowledge of history and society is poor and their understanding of illness is lacking in depth They are wed to a materialistic mentality: man is a body and his illnesses are treated with synthetic molecules. Of course, this is a mistake, but how will the medical profession regain its stature as a profession and its vision of the whole man if it fails to engage in its ranks men and women with a good liberal arts education?

Dentistry is a long-standing profession, an art and a science that continues to develop its capacity for treatment of various illnesses. Like medicine and nursing, it requires a special dedication and respect for patients that inform the professional relationship.

Nursing and Pharmacology, two professions integral to healthcare, both require extensive study of biology and medicine, where the former has a strong humanistic component. Nurses care for the sick; patients depend on nurses for human care, which goes beyond the physiological treatments. They understand, console and guide patients and their families. They accompany them through suffering and also at the time of death. Both are noble professions that call for a great deal of study and dedication. Since nursing is commonly a second career path, many universities offer accelerated programs for registered nurses, for which a bachelor in liberal arts would provide an excellent foundation.

Law is one of the oldest professions; the first medieval university started as a school of law in Bologna. The liberal arts prepare students well for this profession, which has a very wide range of application in private and public law. This field can boast of a number of saints: Thomas More, Lord Chancellor of England under King Henry VIII, Alphonsus Ligouri, bishop and noted author on the spiritual life and on Christian morality, and Bartolo Longo, founder of a Marian shrine and a school for orphans in Pompei. The legal profession, today more than ever, needs men and women of character, who will promote and defend the common good in civil life, beginning with respect for the life of every innocent human being. The study of philosophy and theology in liberal arts programs prepare future lawyers for the requisite understanding of the common good and justice.

The Social Sciences make up a large group of disciplines in the university that provide multiple avenues of professional work. These sciences include political science, psychology, anthropology, economics and sociology. Graduate studies in political science vary greatly in their political and philosophical orientation from university to university, depending on university faculty appointments. Plato rightly thought that a good ruler should be a philosopher king, indicating by this the need for rulers to exercise prudence and justice. The study of political philosophy and civic virtues is thus important for lawyers, civil servants and policy makers in government. As in law, the foundations of a good liberal arts education are very beneficial for political science.

Economics, in its present mathematical form, is one the most recent social sciences. Although business schools are a 20th century development, the practice of business goes back to prehistoric man. In the 16th century, some Spanish theologians in Salamanca made an important contribution to economics and modern law with their discussions and treatises on commerce, just interest rates and international laws. Business schools have become an established part of contemporary universities. Unfortunately, the model is one that extols the free market economy with its supposed self-regulation without a natural law framework of the person and society. As much as these schools excel in management, finance and leadership training, they lack a vision of the common good espoused in the Catholic Church's social doctrine and most recently in Benedict XVI's encyclical letter *Caritas in Veritate*. It is of little surprise that some top business school programs do not include business ethics. In those schools where business ethics is taught, it is not an ethics based on ethical principles derived through reason enlightened by faith. It is almost always an ethics based on legality, consensus and informed consent. A Catholic who wishes to make business his career has to take seriously the study of business ethics and apply the natural law principles to his work with the help of like-minded Christians.

The Natural Sciences make up the other very significant part of modern universities, and a large number of students go to college for the sake of working in a vast number of research labs and institutions. Many students go on to graduate work in biology, molecular biology, chemistry and physics. Of these, many wish to obtain faculty positions in basic or applied research. As discussed in an earlier chapter, empirical fields of study have their own specific methodologies based predominantly on inductive reasoning. This type of reasoning is very different from the deductive reasoning of theology. It is important for anyone doing graduate work in these fields to have a healthy respect for the conclusions of theology in matters that are proper to it, limiting their conclusions to what is proper to the object of study and methods of natural sciences. An undergraduate liberal arts education or some knowledge of liberal arts helps them to avoid an unnecessary conflict between science and faith.

Engineering is not graduate education *per se*, but is a professional study in which, unlike other professions, students enroll directly following high school. After completing one year or so of general requirements in humanities, they major in engineering. Graduates from these programs, for the most part, know about engineering but have a weak humanistic formation. Many do not miss this or see the point in it. They would prefer to have even more time to learn more science rather than fulfill some general requirements. Students who wish to have a complete university education and are able to afford it might consider obtaining a degree in liberal arts and afterwards applying to an engineering school. Since many students choose not to follow this path or are unable to do so it would be preferable that engineering schools pay more attention to the quantity and quality of their humanities requirements.

Architecture, like engineering, is an undergraduate program, usually a five-year degree that combines architectural theory and structural design with construction methodology. Architects create public and private spaces: houses, offices and buildings in which families live and people work. They seek beauty and functionality without sacrificing one or the other. Architects therefore need to have a good humanistic formation that permits them to understand human beings, their needs and traditions, their desire for beauty and need for communication with others.

Our strip malls and shopping centers do not seem designed for people and families to come together in a public space; the first lack beauty, the second conceive man as a consumer only. Architects as well as city planners and developers play a role in creating spaces conducive to social life and work; they therefore need a spiritual vision of man. The communist buildings of Eastern Europe exemplify the failure of an architecture that is soulless, the materialism of an ideology closed to the spirit and religion.

Education Science is one of the favorite fields of graduate studies. At Harvard, education is the most popular area of study for graduate students. Teaching and school administration prepare college graduates for work that offers a meaningful contribution to society, although it is usually poorly compensated. Education schools at universities are also strongly influenced by philosophical views on education. Candidates for graduate programs in education must find out what views are espoused and if there is tolerance for other views. A background in humanities gives future teachers and administrators an indispensable strong grounding in the classical principles of education.

The Humanities are mentioned last, not because of their lesser importance but because of their relation to the future of society, the subject of the last paragraphs of this chapter. These include philosophy, theology, literature, history, art and archeology. These disciplines, except for archeology, which dates its beginnings to the Renaissance, are the liberal arts that gave origin to the universities in Greece and later in Medieval Europe. Although these disciplines are the real foundation for all university learning, they have been displaced by the social sciences and natural sciences. The humanities look to the past whereas the social sciences and natural sciences look to the future. The former do not seem to provide answers whereas the latter, especially the natural sciences, produce practical and quantifiable results. This, however, is not true; the humanities continue to provide men with the indispensable foundations for all human activities.

Philosophy is, as considered for centuries, the queen of the sciences, giving the necessary architectonic order to the rest. Modern and contemporary philosophies have not been able to eclipse ancient philosophy completely but, with their emphasis on the mind, have forgotten the objective realism of the Aristotelian-Thomistic philosophy. They have also often reduced the philosophical questions to matters of language and theory of knowledge. The great challenge of today's graduate students and future professors of philosophy is a rediscovery and teaching of Socrates, Plato and Aristotle together with the insights of philosophers throughout the ages. The philosopher has the task of helping students and people at large to ask the fundamental questions in life and to point to meaningful answers that admit of universal truths.

Theology was one of the schools in the medieval universities and remains a fundamental discipline and profession for society. In addition to the need for priests well trained in theology, laypersons are needed to teach this discipline in high schools, colleges and universities. They are needed to continue the work of research in the many fields of theology. Yet, for theology to assert its guiding role in society, especially in the university and the Church, it must return to a humble understanding and acceptance of its dependence on Tradition and the Sacred Scriptures under the guidance of the Church's Magisterium.

The work of historians, both academic and popular, bears a lot of influence on culture and society. Historians need to have the intellectual honesty of telling history without falling into ideologies such as those of the Enlightenment or Marxism that have given us a revisionist history. Newman admired Edward Gibbons' erudition and literary style but strongly criticized his anti-Catholic writing of history. Historians need, perhaps more than others, the philosophical habit of discriminating between facts and opinions, arriving at the most impartial judgments possible while offering plausible explanations for events and developments in history. High school history teachers have the opportunity and obligation to teach new generations what we can learn from the past, examining different beliefs and ideas with fairness. Today more than ever before, students must learn what Chesterton called the "democracy of the dead," that is, the tradition and wisdom of past generations.[140]

Careers in Languages and Literature are paramount for society because ideas and culture are conveyed through the written word in prose and poetry. A revival of the study of the classics will contribute greatly to the promotion of the values of western civilization. There is also the need for teachers who can teach the great authors of modern literature, also allowing these authors to speak for themselves, transmitting the wisdom of ages rather than doing a partial and skewed reading that fits with contemporary ideas on sex or freedom. English teachers have the challenge of bringing literacy to a generation of youth made illiterate by the mass media and contemporary action movies. Foreign language teachers are needed to open the American mind so often closed to the cultural and intellectual heritage of other nations. From among those dedicated to

---

[140] "Tradition means giving a vote to most obscure of all classes, our ancestors. It is the democracy of the dead. Tradition refuses to submit to the small and arrogant oligarchy of those who merely happen to be walking about. All democrats object to men being disqualified by the accident of birth; tradition objects to their being disqualified by the accident of death. Democracy tells us not to neglect a good man's opinion, even if he is our groom; tradition asks us not to neglect a good man's opinion, even if he is our father." G. K. Chesterton, *Orthodoxy*, chapter 4, http://www.gutenberg.org/files/16769/16769-h/16769-h.htm, accessed on December 21, 2014.

language and literature will come forth the writers, novelists and journalists who can inspire men and women.

One last and very important group of professions for society consists in the wide field of the Arts, including fine arts, dance and music. There is a long and rich heritage of art, in both the East and the West that delights and expresses the history of cultures. Newer forms of art such as large musical concerts and movies with their wide appeal, as well as the older forms, elicit the questions: What is man? What is art? What is beauty? Study of the liberal arts provides artists with the classical philosophy of man and philosophy of beauty that can help them to channel their artistic expression. In particular, there is need for a rediscovery of the transcendentals, namely *one, truth, goodness* and *beauty*, and the classical notion of beauty, which Thomas Aquinas defined as that which gives pleasure when seen.[141] For the Dominican saint, beauty has four properties or standards: actuality[142], proportion, radiance and integrity.[143] How far art has strayed from the form, the essence of things, through a long history of contemporary art that led to modern abstract art and finally to decadent art. This is a reflection of the loss of the classical humanities and its understanding of the human being, a challenge to artists in all mediums.

Future Generations

So far, we have considered some paths open to those who study liberal arts in college. There are other very important considerations on what follows a liberal arts degree. This type of education is integral to raising a family, educating successive generations. We must ask ourselves, "Who will educate the next and future generations?"

---

[141] Thomas Aquinas, *Summa Theologiae,* I-II, Q. 27, a. 1.
[142] Aquinas does not mention "actuality" in the list of characteristics of beauty, but for him everything is rooted in its "actuality" or being so that being is the basis for beauty. "Medieval Theories of Aesthetics," *Internet Encyclopedia of Philosophy,* accessed on November 14, 2014 from www.iep.utm.edu/m-aesthe/#SH1b
[143] Aquinas, *Summa Theologiae,* I, Q. 39, a. 8 c.

Naturally, men and women need to support themselves and their families. Those needs, however, are not only material, they are spiritual. Children need a balanced and integral education, and what better preparation for this task than a solid foundation in the liberal arts? This makes the investment of time and resources of a college education more than worthwhile.

The virtues forged through the reading and discussion of great literature with friends and teachers, the ideas considered in philosophy and theology courses and the understanding gained from the course of history is what enables young men and women to teach their children to think and develop as human beings. They can only transmit to their children and grandchildren what they have studied and reflected upon. The best of western thought and tradition is the treasure that they can share with their family and future generations. The culture of violent movies and senseless video games has all but replaced the tradition of storytelling, poetry recitation, writing and listening to music.

The liberal arts form men and women to be responsible members of society. As much as society needs businessmen and engineers, it needs humanists and statesmen steeped in western culture who can help direct the course of society, preserving and fostering its institutions and finding solutions to the social and moral problems of every age.

A mistaken and partly discredited notion of progress advanced in the 1960's holds that mankind will solve the problems of the world through science and technological solutions. This mindset considers man's problems to be merely technical problems. Once these are solved, people think, everything will be fine and there will be happiness and peace in the world. A similar viewpoint is that problems can be solved with money: if you put enough money into solving problems, you will solve them. Both of these views also hold that the solution to the world's problems is a question of providing education for people. Even if this were true, one would need to ask, "what type of education remedies divisions and war?"

When these ideas were advanced in the England of his time, Newman replied that men are not made moral by libraries or science. Instead, men are made moral through religious instruction and the effort to grow in virtue. Here it must be explained that not even a liberal arts education is sufficient.

> "Liberal Education makes not the Christian, not the Catholic, but the gentleman. It is well to be a gentlemen, it is well to have a cultivated intellect, a delicate taste, a candid, equitable, dispassionate mind, a noble and courteous bearing in the conduct of life;—these are the connatural qualities of a large knowledge; they are the objects of a University; I am advocating, I shall illustrate and insist upon them; but still, I repeat, they are no guarantee for sanctity or even for conscientiousness, they may attach to the man of the world, to the profligate, to the heartless,—pleasant, alas, and attractive as he shows when decked out in them."

These qualities in themselves do not constitute virtue. They are admired and, in themselves, contribute to civil life, but they are unable to make men moral. For this, men and women have to learn morality and train their passions. This work of formation relies heavily on the personal influence of others. We help others become men or women of character through our personal example and advice. Christian friendship is a vital part of the transmission of faith and culture. Newman advocated a Christian humanism through his friendship and letters, even though this was not a term that he used. Instead, he used the term "personal influence" to denote the power of Christian friendship. Some of his close friends and students became lords in Parliament, were recognized lawyers, or held other high positions of government. They often sought Newman's advice and prayers for matters that came before them. He aided them to exercise prudence and fortitude in their decisions, and to advance Christian ideals in society and the service of the Church.

Well-formed Christians will strive to shape culture and its manifold expressions: the economy, music, arts, teaching, science and other manifestations. They will draw from history and tradition, and guide men to make moral decisions about the present and the future. They will meet a lot of resistance. Without the necessary moral formation and respect for the human person, however, some scientists and rulers will make possible the creation of new atom bombs and in-vitro human beings. Those scientists who envision that their discoveries can be used for destructive purposes must have the courage to oppose such use, as some have done. Guided by ethical principles other scientists, such as Shinya Yamanaka and his collaborators, who developed the technique for producing induced pluripotent stem cells, will spare the destruction of human embryos for the procurement of embryonic stem cells. Thus, metaphysics, moral philosophy, religion and other aspects of a liberal arts education are vital for the health and future of society, for a true understanding of goodness and justice.

Plato reflected on this many centuries ago. At the end of The Parable of the Cave in *The Republic,* the prisoner sees the light of day outside of the cave and recognizes the sun as the lord of the visible world. He does not wish to return to the cave where there are only shadows. Yet he is taken back to be with his fellow prisoners who scoff at him because, due to the ascent, he has lost his sight. Once the philosopher has been educated and turned his soul from the realm of becoming towards that of being then he has experienced the *To Agathon* (the good), he must descend to the *polis* to educate others. He is under the stern decree: "Down you must go (*katabateon*)."[144]

What follows after college and a liberal arts degree is therefore very personal, but a student's liberal arts education prior to professional studies has a significant bearing on society as a whole, beginning with the future of families. A shortsighted view would only look at the immediate applicability of a liberal arts degree and its questionable financial return. It would consider liberal arts as a delay or setback in professional goals, but as the aforementioned considerations indicate, this is not true. A real liberal arts education sets the stage for a meaningful professional career, and leads men and women along a path to happiness and wisdom. Students, especially those who are more gifted and have greater opportunities to go on to higher education, must rebel from the easy profession-focused approach to college or university studies. They must aspire

---

[144] Plato, *Republic,* 520c. This recalls the opening of the *Republic* where Socrates went down from the city of Athens to the port of Piraeus for a festival in honor of Bendis, a foreign goddess. He said: "I went down (*kateben*), 327a.

to intellectual and moral greatness, and make a difference in the society in which they live. They should heed the founder of the University of Navarre, St. Josemaría Escrivá, who challenged each university student: "Don't let your life be sterile. Be useful. Blaze a trail. Shine forth with the light of your faith and of your love."[145]

Recommended Reading:

Allan Bloom. *The Closing of the American Mind: How Higher Education has Failed Democracy and Impoverished the Souls of Today's Students.* New York: Simon & Schuster, 1987. 336-382.

Boethius, *The Consolation of Philosophy,* trans. and ed. by Scott Goins and Barbara H. Wyman. San Francisco: Ignatius Press, 2012.

Plato. *Republic.* 514-520c-d; For an explanation of the parable see Eric Voegelin, *Order and History, Vol. III: Plato and Aristotle.* Louisianna: Louisiana State University Press, 1957. 114-117.

---

[145] St. Josemaría Escrivá, *The Way* (New York: Scepter Press, 2006), n 1.

Through this book we hope to have provided an answer to the questions posed in the prologue: "What is a good college education?" and "How do I get this kind of education?" By way of recapitulation, we recall some of the main ideas put forth to answer these and other questions.

The minds of Americans - and we could add, that of other western men and women - have been closed by a cultural relativism that denies the superiority of western culture over other world cultures, and by a marked emphasis on the study of only what is useful knowledge, to the detriment of the development of a philosophical habit of mind or perfection of the intellect, where perfection is not to be understood as "the best" in a group but the natural goal of the faculties of a being.

Colleges and universities have lost their identity as true educational institutions and their sense of mission: the cultivation of the mind of their students. The contemporary university is a disjointed collection of schools and departments without a common vision of man and society, once provided by Christian thought. The result is the fragmentation of knowledge and university studies that provide students with many facts in one or another discipline but little understanding about the relationship between the knowledge reached in various disciplines, and few or no answers to the fundamental questions about life and its meaning.

The Liberal Arts, once the foundation for university education, have been replaced in most schools by political and ideological study programs focused on sex, race and gender. Students fulfill their minimal general education requirements with courses that lack academic rigor and substance, and that ignore or reject classical western thought.

Over the last few centuries and especially the 20th century, the growth and triumph of experimental sciences has resulted in an exaggerated and unchecked faith in progress and the reduction of reason to scientific knowledge. This impoverishment of knowledge has left most people bereft or unsure of the knowledge that is gained through philosophy and theology, literature and fine arts, and the wisdom received from different cultures.

Institutions of higher learning have a serious responsibility for the future of society. But few of these institutions offer persons the education needed for their human growth and perfection as whole human beings and responsible members of society. Instead, most colleges and universities train students in very specific tasks while rewarding selfish desires of individual success. Society desperately needs future thinkers and leaders who will be able to address the world's problems of unemployment, illness, war, lack of meaning and loss of religious faith. For the most part, only a good college or university education can provide students with the necessary intellectual and moral formation.

The opening of the mind of future leaders, the condition for the true progress of a society, requires a renewed vision of the university by educators and administrators. University faculties must recover a unitary vision of the disciplines and a hierarchical structuring of same. Students need help to ask and find answers to the fundamental questions of life. Within this vision, the study of natural theology as well as revealed theology and the study of western classics should occupy a central role. A rediscovery of the harmony between science and faith and of the proper autonomy of disciplines is another pressing need and challenge for both scientists and theologians who educate the future generations of students.

Those university presidents and professors who value western culture and understand its indispensable contribution to university education must have the valor to fight to the end to restore or at least improve the education imparted at colleges and universities. They could well be inspired by the account of Hector's prayer for his son in Homer's *Iliad.* As Hector is about to go out of the gates of Troy to defend it from the attacks of the Achaeans, and ultimately die, he bids goodbye to his wife and child. Removing his plumed helmet, which scares his child, and raising him in his arms, Hector prays to Jove and all the gods: "... let him be not less excellent in strength, and let him rule Ilius with his might."[146]

---

[146] The passage continues: "Then may one say of him as he comes

143

It is on all accounts desirable that new magnanimous men and women rise, both within and outside of institutions of higher education, who like Hector's child can transmit the torch of liberal learning and advance it. However, since relatively few university presidents and faculty adhere to the aforementioned vision of knowledge and the formation of the soul, such a change will only occur in some schools, and thus students and parents must find the universities with the best liberal arts programs that also fit their other financial and personal needs.

They should realize the importance of classic western thought and try to obtain the foundations of a liberal arts education, either by majoring in liberal arts or at least by choosing courses that fulfill their general education requirements from a classical core curriculum. Following the latter, science majors too will acquire some of the important concepts and principles of Western thought.

This view of higher education and the corresponding study is an enriching path for the growth of the person and society, and it overcomes the shortsighted attempt to teach professions to undergraduates before they have developed a good habit of thinking (a sound capacity for understanding, comparing and judging about things).

As Bishop James D. Conley writes: "Good literature forms a worldview: it offers us insight into our families, our communities, and our selves. Great literature offers us insight into our relationship with God and the world."[147] Students as well as college graduates will

---

from battle, 'The son is far better than the father.' May he bring back the blood-stained spoils of him whom he has laid low, and let his mother's heart be glad.'" Homer, *Iliad*, Bk VI.

[147] Bishop James D. Conley, "Sursum Corda: Ten Suggestions for Rekindling the Literary Imagination," in publication. The essay begins: "Great men and women—great souls—are formed by great literature. Abraham Lincoln, Theodore Roosevelt, and Thomas Jefferson were voracious readers. St. Paul, St. Augustine and St. Thomas Aquinas were steeped in the literary traditions of their times. St. John Paul II, canonized just last year, recalls that in his

learn from important 20th century novelists, philosophers and theologians who were Christians and whose works form part of a good liberal arts education. A partial list of these authors, some of them mentioned or quoted in these pages, should include Leo Tolstoy, Hugh Benson, Sigrid Undset, Willa Cather, Evelyn Waugh, G. K. Chesterton, C. S. Lewis, Jacques and Raïssa Maritain, Romano Guardini, Yves Congar, Henri de Lubac, Etienne Gilson, Joseph Pieper, Josemaría Escrivá, John Paul II, Benedict XVI, Dietrich and Alice von Hildebrand, Christopher Dawson, Peter Kreeft, James V. Schall, Scott Hahn and others.

From beginning to end, this essay has been guided by the ideas articulated by that great educator and priest, Cardinal John Henry Newman. Accordingly, we wish to close these pages with a quote from his last discourse prior to establishing the Catholic University of Ireland. This long passage serves as a summary, or better, as an enunciation of his various theses, and recapitulates much of the central ideas of this book. We take the liberty of dividing it to highlight the import of its content:

"I have accordingly laid down first, that all branches of knowledge are, at least implicitly, the subject-matter of its teaching; that these branches are not isolated and independent one of another, but form together a whole or system; that they run into each other, and complete each other, and that, in proportion to our view of them as a whole, is the exactness and trustworthiness of the knowledge which they separately convey;

"that the process of imparting knowledge to the intellect in this philosophical way is its true culture; that such culture is a good in itself; that the knowledge which is both its instrument and result is called Liberal Knowledge;

"that such culture, together with the knowledge which effects it, may fitly be sought for its own sake; that it is, however, in addition, of great secular utility, as constituting the best and

youth, he was "completely consumed by a passion for literature."

highest formation of the intellect for social and political life
(...)"[148]

With these principles in mind, Newman found teachers, prepared study plans, sought the enrollment of students and planned for residential halls (colleges). Then on November 3, 1854, the evening before the Catholic University opened, he told the first seventeen students that they had not come to become doctors, engineers, soldiers, bankers or businessmen, since they could receive this professional education elsewhere. Instead, they had come to the university 'to be made men'.[149] Their undergraduate education was for the enlargement of the mind and formation of character; it was not primarily a preparation for a career. Such is the result of the cultivation of the soul, its intellect and will, through the teaching of professors and the sharing of a community of friends. This liberal education is a great privilege, a great challenge and great responsibility for oneself and for the common good.

---

[148] Newman, "Discourse 8: Knowledge Viewed in Relation to Religion," *Idea of a University,* 214.

[149] Shrimpton, *The 'Making of Men,' The Idea and Reality of Newman's university in Oxford and Dublin,* 175-176. The author quotes Newman's words in an *Address to the students on the opening of the University* (November 1854) from *My Campaign in Ireland,* 314-315.

APPENDIX A: Questions to Ask Before Applying to a College or University

Answers to these questions can be found by looking at good college guides such as *Choosing the Right College: 2014-2015* and by speaking with college graduates, looking at school websites or visiting campuses.

Academics and Administration

Are there outstanding professors teaching there? Do these professors teach undergraduates or do they focus primarily on research?

Do mostly graduate students do the teaching?

Is there an environment of free speech and respect among professors and students?

Are the requirements for general education good or are they lax?

Does the school offer a good amount of liberal arts courses or is it focused on natural sciences or specialized studies?

Is there an honors program?

Do humanities courses focus on sex, race and gender? Are departments politicized?

Is there a good philosophy department with courses on the Ancient Greeks and Thomas Aquinas?

Does the school offer good Catholic theology courses? On the contrary, is there a predominance of courses on non-Christian religions?

Is there respect for the religious beliefs of students and faculty? Is there a strong anti-Catholic bias in the school?

Student Life

Is there an intellectual environment among the students?

Are the students and staff welcoming?

Is the school population conducive to meeting people or is it too large?

Is the school free of a reputation for drug abuse or excessive alcohol consumption?

Does the school have single-sex halls/dormitories?

Is there a culture of promiscuity and homosexuality on campus? Does the administration aggressively promote this type of behavior, diversity and "safe sex"?

Is the school campus safe?

Catholic Chaplaincy

Are there small group Catechism and Bible study groups on campus?

Is there weekly Mass and adoration of the Blessed Sacrament?

Is sacramental Confession available on a regular basis?

Does the chaplaincy organize lectures on Catholic thought or Church history?

Does it promote pro-life activities and social initiatives?

Finances

Is the cost for tuition and board affordable?

What is the likely sum to be obtained from grants or scholarships?

What will be the total debt after four years?

Is the financial aid office helpful?

APPENDIX B: First Medieval Universities and their Origins

The university is an ancient institution with a rich history which it is well worthwhile for us to recall in these pages for various reasons: one being a better understanding of the continuity of today's university with classical western civilization, and another a greater appreciation of the very important contribution of the Catholic Church to the genesis of the medieval university, predecessor of the contemporary university. This chapter is a summary of Newman's essays on the history of universities, *The Rise and Progress of Universities*.[150] His sources include the various texts of historians such as Venerable Bede, Bulaeus, Fleury, Döllinger, and the writings of popes. Newman's intent was to draw with some large brush strokes a picture of the "organic growth and development of the university," rather than to write a detailed history.[151]

Newman began with an essay painting a picture of the origins of the university in Athens, Alexandria, and the Roman schools. In the 4th century BC, Greek philosophers gave rise to various small schools in Athens of which the Academy, the Peripatetic (Lyceum) and Stoa stand out. Although independent, together they could be considered the University of Athens. In Alexandria, under the auspices of the Ptolemaic dynasty a much larger university arose which had various special characteristics: a library that housed thousands of books (papyrus), and researchers in the natural sciences. The immense library attracted teachers and students to the Alexandrian university. These teachers and students came from every part of the world; some were chosen by "concursus" or competition. With time, new colleges were added to the original museum. Youths attended lectures in grammar, rhetoric, poetry, philosophy, astronomy, music, medicine and other arts and sciences.

The intellectual environment brought together at one time philosophers, theologians and natural scientists. Some of the great Christian writers and doctors: Clement, Origen, Anatolius,

---

[150] John Henry Newman, *The Rise and Progress of Universities* in *Historical Sketches*, Vol III. London: Longmans, Green, and Co., 1909.
[151] Shrimpton, *The 'Making of Men,' The Idea and Reality of Newman's university in Oxford and Dublin*, 119. Also see p. 165, footnote n. 22.

Athanasius and St. Gregory of Nyssa lived in Alexandria. Ammonius and Plotinus gave rise to neo-Platonism. Among its poets was Apollonius of Rhodes, known for his poem on the Argonauts. Egyptian, Carthaginian and Etruscan antiquities were the subject of research although the fame for Alexandria's medicine and mathematics was far greater. Galen who came from Pergamon was one of its celebrated physicians. Three of the great ancient mathematicians also taught in Alexandria: Apollonius of Perga, Diophantus, a native Alexandrian, and Euclid whose country is unknown. Apollonius wrote on conic sections and Diophantus on algebra. Other illustrious men who lived in Alexandria were Eratosthenes of Cyrene, and Ptolemy, said to be of Pelusium, for whom the Ptolemaic system is named.

Schools also arose in the Roman Empire but the approach in Rome and its colonies was different from that of Alexandria. The Roman schools run by the government were for younger students and, for the most part, these had a practical purpose, the formation of government officials. The Roman Senate at first succeeded in expelling philosophers from Rome and precluded the start of schools of philosophy from starting, but ultimately, philosophers won and schools were gradually founded in Rome and in every great city of the Empire. The schools of Marseilles, Bordeaux, Autun and Rheims enjoyed a high reputation, as did the one in Milan. The *Trivium* and *Quadrivium* were taught in these schools.

The emperors established the Roman University, today called Sapienza, which had chairs for Latin Grammar and Rhetoric as well as Greek Grammar and Rhetoric. There were chairs also for Philosophy and Roman Law. A professorship of Medicine was added later on. Roman Law was taught in Rome, Constantinople and Berytus. Newman offers more details:

> "The study of grammar and geography was commenced at the age of twelve, and apparently at the private school, and was continued till the age of fourteen. Then the youths were sent to the public academy for oratory, philosophy, mathematics, and law. The course lasted five years; and, on entering on their twentieth year, their education was considered complete, and they were sent home."

Students of law and fine arts were allowed to continue until the age of 25. Youths traveled from Africa and Gaul to study law. They were carefully supervised to avoid the moral dangers of Rome. They required a certificate from the magistrate of their province, and a "censuales" or proctor of sorts ensured that their lodging in the city, studies and conduct were in order. If their conduct was not upright, they were subjected to public punishment and expulsion to their country of origin.

Education was oriented for civil administration where useful knowledge was more important than the fine arts. This vast organization of schools saw its demise with the invasion of successive Barbarian tribes.

Irish Monasteries

In the 3rd and 4th centuries AD, the early Goths (Visigoths) invaded the eastern portion of the Roman Empire but were vanquished by the civilization which they had conquered; they assimilated Roman culture. Soon afterwards, however, they were defeated by other Barbarians. In the 5th century AD, the Huns, under Attila, destroyed Roman civilization, and the Lombards, who followed the Huns initially, did the same with even greater fury.

Pope Gregory (590-604) lamented the destruction that befell the empire by the sword, a plague lasting many years, and a succession of earthquakes in Constantinople, Antioch and Berytus. Rome and every city had public libraries; Rome alone had twenty-nine.[152] The Barbarians destroyed these libraries and sacked the monasteries. Architecture, engineering and agriculture fell into ruin and were swallowed up by wilderness. In the face of such natural calamities and invasions, the popes asked: "What is coming? What is to be the end?(...) What could be done for art, science, and philosophy, when towns had been burned up, and country devastated?"[153]

The popes looked for a place where learning could be cultivated, and they turned their attention to the north, just beyond the limits of the

---

[152] Rise and Progress, 111-112.
[153] Idem. 114.

Roman world, to Ireland and Britannia, instead of Alexandria. There the Catholic Church preserved a great part of learning and culture. Christianity had been present in Britain since the 3rd century, but a new evangelization of the Anglo-Saxons ensued when St. Gregory sent St. Augustine[154] and a large group of Benedictine monks to Christianize King Æthelbert and his kingdom of Kent. Christianity arrived in Ireland before the 5th century, but it expanded with the work of St. Patrick sent there by Pope Celestine (ca 432). The Church soon flourished in Ireland.

According to Church historian Döllinger, during the 6th and 7th centuries the Church of Ireland blossomed at all levels of society. The most celebrated schools in all of the West arose in Irish cloisters. Among these were St. Finian's of Clonard, founded in 530, and Cataldus, founded in 640. Monks traveled from the continent and later from England to Ireland to learn from the ascetical practices of the Irish monks and to study the Scriptures. From Ireland, they went to England to found monasteries or to take the Gospel to the German Saxons.[155]

From Ireland, the monks also carried the Gospel to various parts of Europe. St. Columba founded the famous monastery of Iona on the northwestern coast of Scotland (ca 563); and Aidan, a monk from Iona, founded the monastery of Lindisfarne in 634 on the island by that name in Northumbria (today northern England and southeastern Scotland). St. Fridolin worked in France as far as the Rhine, and St. Columbanus traveled to France, Burgundy, Switzerland and Lombardy.

The Irish missionaries also evangelized parts of Anglo-Saxon England. The Venerable Bede (672-735) praised the piety, zeal and material detachment of the Irish bishops, monks and priests in Northumbria. These Irish monastic schools thus preserved learning and civilization in the West, a work to be continued by the English monks.

---

[154] This is a reference to St. Augustine of Canterbury thus known because he became the first Archbishop of Canterbury in 597.
[155] Rise and Progress, 127.

In 668, Pope Vitalian, who followed closely the ecclesiastical affairs of England, consecrated Theodore of Tarsus, a highly educated monk living in Rome, for the See of Canterbury. He wished to unite the people of England and maintain a close tie with Rome. The pope sent with him Adrian, another learned monk to be the head of the monastery at Canterbury.

Newman writes how "Passing through France, in their way to their post of duty, these monks delayed there a while at the command of the Pope, to accustom themselves to the manners of the North; and at length they made their appearance in England, with a collection of books, Greek classics, and Gregorian chants, and whatever other subjects of study may be considered to fill up the interval between those two." These men founded schools for both secular and sacred learning in the south of England.

Newman asserts that glory of the Irish Church was followed by the glory of the Anglo-Saxon Church, and he masterfully describes the work of the missionaries.

> "The seventh and eighth centuries are the glory of the Anglo-Saxon Church, as are the sixth and seventh of the Irish. As the Irish missionaries travelled down through England, France, and Switzerland, to lower Italy, and attempted Germany at the peril of their lives, converting the barbarian, restoring the lapsed, encouraging the desolate, collecting the scattered, and founding churches, schools, and monasteries, as they went along; so, amid the deep pagan woods of Germany and round about, the English Benedictine plied his axe and drove his plough, planted his rude dwelling and raised his rustic altar upon the ruins of idolatry, and then settling down as a colonist upon the soil, began to sing his chants and to copy his old volumes, and thus to lay the slow but sure foundations of the new civilization."[156]

---

[156] Idem, 128.

According to Newman, both nations had a different character and talent; the Irish resembling more the Greek, and the Anglo-Saxons, the Romans, yet both boasted a very long list of scholars and saints. The impressive record of the Irish and English Church is a tribute to the hard work and ideal of holiness of the monasteries and their monks, to their missionary zeal and preservation of learning. For most people, it is an unheard story or, at best, a forgotten one that must be retold.

Charlemagne's Schools

When in 800 Charlemagne rose to power on the continent, becoming emperor, the Danes began to descend upon Britain and Ireland islands. The mission of two islands, to preserve learning, was at an end. Relating this, however, Newman notes that it was the Anglo-Saxon Alcuin and the Irish Clement who were the first and second rectors of the *Studium* of Paris. In the same period, it was the Irish John Scotus (Eriugena) who founded the school of Pavia, and the Irish Dungall, a monk of St. Denis, who defeated the heretical iconoclasm of Bishop Claudius of Turin.[157]

During the late Roman Empire, the Church taught the clergy but the laity were educated for the most part in state schools. When the Roman Empire collapsed, the Church began to educate both clergy and laity. Newman writes: "Henceforth, as all government, so all education, was to be founded on Revealed Truth. Secular teaching was to be united to sacred; and the Church had the supervision both of lay students and of profane learning."

Charlemagne undertook a great work of promoting education and culture, choosing Alcuin, an Englishman, to set up schools of sacred and profane learning in the Frankish Empire. Charlemagne laid down the principles for universities as we know them, institutions open to all classes of students and teaching all subjects. He first paid attention to the restoration of Episcopal seminaries, places of training for future clergy, which had suffered from the Barbarian invasions. These institutions would last for four centuries when they were absorbed by universities. In the 16th century, the Council of

---

[157] Idem, 129.

Trent once again made them independent. In addition to seminaries, he added grammar and public schools.

He wished to establish two kinds of schools, the lesser and the greater. The lesser were to reside in bishops' places and monasteries; the greater were for public places and for the education of students of every rank and class. He found examples of large public schools in the ancient schools of Athens, Alexandria, Rome, Constantinople and Berytus. In the Benedictine monasteries, he found examples for both kind of institutions. Laymen were also educated in the monasteries, but many of the most clever embraced the monastic life, and kings were obliged to seek monks to run the civil administration.

Accordingly, Charlemagne wished for lesser schools to be set up or retained in bishops' palaces. Instead, he sought the creation of three schools of higher and public learning in important cities in his empire: Paris, Pavia and Bologna.

The development of Catholic medieval universities occurred over the span of a number of centuries. It was a great enterprise that revived the ancient institutions of learning of Athens and Alexandria but under the auspices of the Catholic Church and Catholic monarchs. The Christian confidence in reason and the harmony between reason and faith enabled the development and growth of these institutions.

Newman does not give an account of the period between Charlemagne and the consolidation of the first medieval universities, but he notes that these developed out of the public or grammar schools and the monastic schools. He described it as "a movement" requiring a "comprehensive philosophy." By this, we should understand a confidence in reason and rather a specific philosophical school. The subjects of the universities were the existing *Trivium* (grammar, logic, rhetoric,) and the *Quadrivium* (geometry, astronomy, arithmetic, and music).

> "These were inherited from the ancient world, and were the foundation of the system which was then in course of formation. But the life of Universities lay in the new sciences, not indeed superseding, but presupposing Arts, viz., those of

Theology, Law, Medicine, and in subordination to them, of Metaphysics, Natural History, and the languages."[158]

What were only local centers of learning attracted larger numbers of students and became places with a "systematizing of knowledge."

As the number of students grew, they were divided in groups by nations and a "procrator" or proctor headed each group. At different universities, the heads of the universities were called rector, chancellor or provost. At first, the head of a university taught students, but as the sciences increased, the instruction was left to doctors who taught a given science. This was the origin of deans of faculties. Initially degrees were only a testimonial that a resident was fit to teach at a given university, but once universities were recognized by the state or other universities, then the import of degrees changed. As students mastered subjects, they received the title "magistri" or master, and when they were qualified for teaching, they were given the title "doctoris."

In contrast to the grammar or public schools, only the "schola majores" had medicine, law and theology; these schools were located in the great cities and were few in number. Locations that were salubrious and beautiful were chosen as the site for universities. Another difference between public schools and universities is that popes, emperors and kings were the founders of universities, whereas lesser authorities in church and state were the founders of colleges and schools. Another distinction, according to the greater and lesser schools, was that they differed in their government: the colleges had one head, while the universities were governed by the community of scholars that constituted them.

Bologna and the First Universities

Today most universities, especially in large cities, have foreign students and teachers, but the extent to which this happened in the medieval universities was remarkable given the mode of travel and economic circumstances of that period of history. Newman recounts how the desire and commitment to learning was the impetus for this

---

[158] Idem, 170-171.

exchange of students and teachers, verified in the case of the Universities of Bologna, Oxford, Cambridge and Paris.

Newman writes that Bologna "affords us an observable instance, first, of the self-originating, independent character of the scientific movement,—then, of the influence and attraction it exerted on the people,—and lastly, of the incidental difficulties through which it slowly advanced in the course of many years to its completion."[159]

The University of Bologna was most likely the earliest medieval university. At the end of the 11th century, it had a school of civil law. In the following century, it had one of canon law and, in the 13th, one of grammar and literature, followed some years later by one of theology and another of medicine. That same century, it had ten thousand students, some coming across the sea from England.

In the case of Oxford, the fame of men such as Vacarius, an Italian authority in civil and canon law, and Robert Pullus, a biblical scholar, drew many students; the latter had studied in Paris before teaching at Oxford and later became a cardinal and Chancellor of the Apostolic See.[160] In Cambridge, a similar intellectual movement was taking place, prompted by Jeoffred, or Goisfred, Abbot of Croyland, who sent four French monks to teach in Cambridge. One monk taught sacred verse and the others philosophy. They were so knowledgeable that the barn in which they had begun to teach became insufficient for the students. Newman notes that Scripture verse was taught; only in the 13th century would theology, properly speaking, be taught by the Dominican friars.

The teachers came from afar and did not depend so much on kings but on the enthusiasm they created with their classes. With regard to learning at Paris, Newman quotes the Church historian Fleury:

> "The reputation of the school of Paris (...) increased considerably at the commencement of the twelfth century under William of Champeaux and his disciples at St. Victor's. At the same time Peter Abelard came thither and skilled them

---

[159] Idem, 169.
[160] Idem, 171.

with great éclat the humanities and the Aristotelic philosophy. Alberic of Rheims taught there also; and Peter Lombard, Hildebert, Robert Pullus, the Abbot Rupert, and Hugh of St. Victor; Albertus Magnus also, and the Angelic Doctor."[161]

Something similar had happened three centuries earlier when Charlemagne brought men from Italy, England and Ireland to France. Newman commented on the daring quality of the medieval scholars and masters who traveled far and wide across dangerous waters for the sake of learning and teaching. He offers the example of John of Salisbury who spent twelve years in various lands learning from other scholars, supporting himself by teaching the children of nobles.

Soon there were other universities in Spain, France, Italy, Portugal and later Germany.[162] The centers of learning and talent, however, were in Paris and Oxford. There was an intimate connection between these two centers of learning. Antony Wood, a 17th century Oxford historian, gives a list of thirty-two Oxford professors who taught for some time in Paris. Alexander Hales and St. Edmund, afterwards Archbishop of Canterbury, were counted among them. Bulaeus gives a list of important Englishmen who traveled to Paris to study, a practice that continued until the time of Edward III and the wars with France. In 1209, the University of Oxford had three thousand members, and in 1231, as many as thirty thousand.[163] These included Scottish, Irish, Welsh, French, Spanish, German, Bohemian,

---

[161] Idem, 173.
[162] "Among the earliest universities of this type were the University of Bologna (1088), University of Paris(teach. mid-11th century, recogn. 1150), University of Oxford (teach. 1096, recogn. 1167), University of Modena (1175), University of Palencia (1208), University of Cambridge (1209), University of Salamanca (1218), University of Montpellier (1220), University of Padua (1222), University of Toulouse(1229), University of Orleans (1235), University of Siena (1240), University of Coimbra (1288),University of Pisa (1343), Charles University in Prague(1348), Heidelberg University (1386) and the University of St Andrews (1413) begun as private corporations of teachers and their pupils." http://en.wikipedia.org/wiki/Medieval_university.
[163] Rise and Progress, 177.

Hungarian, and Polish students and their dependents. The number was reduced to fifteen thousand in 1263, and to six thousand in 1360. The great change in numbers was due to wars that brought to an end this free exchange between France and England. This was the end in medieval times of the "ecumenical greatness of universities" and rise of national bodies. The close exchange between England and France, the story of the intimate connection between Oxford and Paris, is an inspiring story of Christian medieval scholarship and teaching.

The case of Ireland was unfortunate and sad. Beginning in the 14th century, numerous attempts by bishops, clergy, Dominicans and Franciscans failed to establish a university. Until that time, thousands of students had studied the *Trivium* and *Quadrivium* at the School of Armagh, but a university with a charter conferring degrees had not been established. There were many reasons for starting such a university, such as the growing national character of universities, facilitating the education of scholars and the expense and dangers of traveling abroad. There were other attempts to establish a university in the 15th century with permission from Parliament and popes. The university failed to get off the ground; some of the attempts failed due to lack of funds.

Colleges and Halls

In a historical sense, colleges are a continuation of the monastic or clerical schools. Although they observed an ecclesiastical rule, they sometimes admitted laymen called externs. This was the case in the early days of the school of Rheims, and also of Bec. As universities developed, monastic orders sought to have colleges for its own members in the universities and to have faculty members in the respective universities. In Paris, in addition to the Dominicans and Franciscans, the Cistercians, Premonstratensians, Carmelites and Benedictines had houses near the university and provided lecturers. Likewise, at Oxford, most of these orders, as well as the Augustinians, had monasteries in the sites of Trinity, Worcester, Beaumont, St. John's and Wadham Colleges.

The monastic orders closed their doors to those who were not monks and thus it became common for laymen to seek out houses where one master, without any assistant tutors, offered a whole course of instruction. This tradition continued and led to the formation of places variously called halls, inns, courts, or hostels. The professor taught and gave board to his students. Universities did not have buildings of their own or endowments. The conditions for poor scholars were dismal, soon prompting a movement to provide housing and scholarships (burses) for them.

Newman quotes a very interesting account of student life from one of the colleges at Cambridge:

> "He (the student) got up between four and five; from five to six he assisted at Mass, and heard an exhortation. He then studied or attended the schools till ten, which was the dinner hour. The meal, which seems also to have been a breakfast, was not sumptuous; it consisted of beef, in small messes for four persons, and a pottage made of its gravy and oatmeal. From dinner to five p.m., he either studied, or gave instruction to others, when he went to supper, which was the principal meal of the day, though scarcely more plentiful than dinner. Afterwards, problems were discussed and other studies pursued, till nine or ten; and then half an hour was devoted to walking or running about, that they might not go to bed with cold feet;—the expedient of hearth or stove for the purpose was out of the question."[164]

Many benefactors established colleges for poor clerks or offered scholarships. As early as 1050, Robert Capet established one for as many as one hundred poor clerks. Other colleges were St. Catherine's in the Valley, founded by St. Louis, the Collegium Bonorum Puerorum, the Harcurianum, or Harcourt College, the College of Navarre in Paris, the Sorbonne and the Montague College. Many diocesan or provincial colleges were founded as well as national ones.

There were graver reasons for establishing colleges, namely, that of providing youth with necessary discipline and moral restraints.

---

[164] Idem, 219.

Like grammar schools, Episcopal schools later also gave rise to the universities. From the 5th century, the Lateran Cathedral in Rome had a school, which also taught literature and had a library. Some of the greatest popes studied there such as St. Gregory II, St. Paul, St. Leo III, St. Paschal, and St. Nicholas. This school continued despite the Barbarian invasions of Italy; in the 13th century, St. Thomas Aquinas and St. Albert the Great lectured in its halls. In other parts of Europe, the teaching at the cathedral schools was interrupted until the revival in education led by Charlemagne.

With the rise of universities, cathedral schools maintained their teaching of secular learning. This was done with the idea that the clergy would not become inferior in learning to the laity or drawn within the influence of universities. The universities, however, drew more students and teachers so that colleges for ecclesiastical students arose in the neighborhood of the universities and cathedral schools ceased to exist. Those who would have studied in seminaries began to live in colleges or lived in the houses of religious orders. Medieval saints, such as St. Raymund, St. John of Matha, St. Thomas of Canterbury, St. Edmund, St. John Nepomucene, St. Cajetan, St. Carlo, St. Ignatius and his companions and St. Francis of Sales, were ordained at universities without seminary training, and by the Council of Trent, seminaries had almost ceased to exist. The candidates for the priesthood had to learn and find religious training on their own.

Danger to the faith and morals of future priests at the universities, fear of the intellectual difficulties posed by biblical and theological questions and, later, the appointment of Protestants to university chairs caused the Council of Trent to restore Episcopal seminaries and suppress ecclesiastical colleges in universities. It allowed for poorer dioceses to unite and establish a provincial seminary, providing sufficient means to offer quality education with a university character. Maynooth College in Ireland and the Seminario Pio in Rome for students from the Papal States, would be examples of this type of seminary.

L'École des Hautes Études in Paris, today L'Institut Catholique, opened in 1845. It was located at the Carmelite convent, the place of the martyrdom of more than a hundred clergymen during the French Revolution. The object of this school was to provide professors for the petits séminaires of France. It was also described as "a novitiate of ecclesiastics intended for teachers of the young clergy." Early on, the students studied languages, literature, history as well as various physical sciences. The institution was like a university and today is also known as the Catholic University of Paris. Laity were admitted for studies and received a sound religious education. Some students went on to studies at the École Polytechnique or other government schools.

Although Newman notes the ebb and flow of history and the power of evil attacking the Church, he had hopes for its educational institutions. With institutions such as L'École des Hautes Études in mind, he confidently wrote: "still we may surely encourage ourselves by a thousand tokens all around us now, that this is our hour, whatever be its duration, the hour for great hopes, great schemes, great efforts, great beginnings. We may live indeed to see but little built, but we shall see much founded. A new era seems to be at hand, and a bolder policy is showing itself."

According to him, in the second half of the 19th century the Church was strong to "recommence the age of Universities." At the time he wrote, Louvain had recently revived and there were prospects for a new University of Paris and a university in Austria, while the Catholic University of Ireland, under his leadership, took its first steps.

As in Newman's time, today the Church and Catholic institutions continue to give life to new universities throughout the world, a sign of its perennial vitality and mission. The challenge remains to maintain the Catholic spirit of the medieval university, which fosters the unity of universal knowledge, while at the same time form the moral lives of its students and prepare them for their work in society.

In *The Rise and Progress of Universities,* Newman enumerated some of the external and internal difficulties faced by colleges and universities, teachers and students, but he did not focus on these with one important exception, the tension during the history of universities between professorial and tutorial systems which in the 19th century were represented by the French universities on the one side and Oxford and Cambridge on the other. He envisioned the Catholic University of Ireland that brought both systems together.[165]

Newman, the historian described the origins in Classical Antiquity of the Medieval University and how the Catholic Church preserved and solidified the inheritance received from Greece and Rome. Furthermore, he demonstrated how the Christian civilization and the Catholic Church fostered and established many medieval universities committed to religious and secular learning, including the natural sciences. Without the medieval university, we would not have today's colleges and universities or its tradition of liberal education. Here lie a number of important lessons from history, ignored by most and untold by others, but always inspiring for those who desire to shape our present and future institutions of higher learning.

---

[165] See Paul Shrimpton, *'The Making of Men,'* 124-127.

"Personal and Literary Character of Cicero" from the Encyclopaedia
     Metropolitana of 1824,
     http://www.newmanreader.org/Works/historical/volume1/
     cicero/index.html

*Holy Scriptures: Book of Wisdom, Gospel of St. John, Letter to the
     Romans.*

Alexis de Tocqueville, *Democracy in America.* New York: The Library
     of America, 2004.

Aristotle, *Nichomachean Ethics, 2nd ed.* Cambridge: Hackett
     Publishing Company Inc, 1999.

Artigas, Mariano and Giberson, Karl. *Oracles of Science: Celebrity
     scientists versus God and religion.* Oxford: Oxford University
     Press, 2006.

Benedict XVI, *Caritas in veritate* [Encyclical Letter on Integral Human
     Development in Charity and Truth]. Accessed on November
     10, 2014.
     http://www.vatican.va/holy_father/benedict_xvi/encyclicals
     /documents/hf_ben-xvi_enc_20090629_caritas-in-
     veritate_en.html

Boethius, *The Consolation of Philosophy*, trans. and ed. by Scott Goins
     and Barbara H. Wyman. San Francisco: Ignatius Press, 2012.

Bloom, Allen. *The Closing of the American Mind: How Higher
     Education has Failed Democracy and Impoverished the Souls of
     Today's Students.* New York: Simon and Schuster, 1987.

Buckley, William F. *God and Man at Yale: the Superstitions of
     'Academic Freedom'.* Washington D.C.: Regnery Publishing,
     1951.

Burgraff, Jutta. *Made for Freedom, Loving, Defending and Living God's
     Gift.* New York: Scepter Publishers, 2012.

Butler, Joseph. *The Analogy of Religion, Natural and Revealed to the Constitution and Court of Nature.* London: John Beecroft, 1771.

Carroll, Colleen. "Campus," *The New Faithful, Why Young Adults are Embracing Christian Orthodoxy.* Illinois: Loyola Press, 2002.

Chaput, Charles. *Catholicism in America: Challenges and Prospects,* ed. Matthew L. Lamb. Florida: Sapientia Press of Ave Maria University, 2012.

Chesterton, C.K. *The Dumb Ox.* South Carolina: CreateSpace Independent Publishing Platform, 2012.

Dawson, Christopher. *Progress and Religion: An Historical Inquiry.* London: Sheed and Ward, 1929.

Drake, Tim. *Young and Catholic: the Face of Tomorrow's Church.* New Hampshire: Sophia Institute Press, 2004.

Escrivá, St. Josemaría. *Conversations with Msgr. Escrivá.* California: Ecclesia Press, 1972.

Escrivá, St. Josemaría. *The Way.* New York: Scepter Press, 2006.

Esposito, Joseph A. *The Newman Guide to Choosing a Catholic College, 2015.* Delaware: ISI Books, 2014.

Flew, Antony. *There is a God, How the World's Most Notorious Atheist Changed His Mind.* HarperOne, 2007.

Gaymard, Clara Lejeune. *Life Is a Blessing: A Biography of Jérôme Lejeune - Geneticist, Doctor, Father.* Philadelphia: National Catholic Bioethics Center, 2011.

Haffner, Paul. "Pitfalls and Prospects of Science," *Creation and Scientific Creativity, A Study in the Thought of J. L. Jaki.* Virginia: Christendom Press, 1991.

Henrie, Mark C. *A Student's Guide to the Core Curriculum.* Delaware: ISI Books, 2000.

Homer. *The Iliad of Homer,* trans. Robert Fagles, Penguin Classics, 1998.

Homer. *The Odyssey of Homer,* trans. Robert Fagles, Penguin Classics, 2006.

Kreeft, Peter. *Because God is Real: Sixteen Questions, One Answer,* San Francisco: Ignatius Press, 2008.

Lewis, C.S. *Mere Christianity,* Harper, 2001.

MacIntyre, Alasdair, *God, philosophy, universities, A Selective History of the Catholic Philosophical Tradition,* New York: Rowman & Littlefield Publishers, Inc, 2009.

McCullough, David. *John Adams.* Simon & Schuster, 2002.

McInerny, Ralph. *I Alone Have Escaped to Tell You: My Life and Pastimes,* South Bend: University of Notre Dame Press, 2011.

Newman, John Henry. *The Idea of a University.* South Bend: University of Notre Dame Press, 1982.

Newman, John Henry. *Historical Sketches.* London: Longmans, Green, and Co., 1909.

Newman, John Henry. *Sermons Preached on Various Occasions,* 13. Accessed on November 10, 2014. http://newmanreader.org/works/occasions/sermon1.html

Newman, John Henry. *Letters and Diaries of John Henry Newman,* ed. Charles Dessain, Edinburgh: Thomas Nelson, 1961.

Newman, John Henry. *My Campaign in Ireland, Part I: Catholic University Reports and Other Papers.* Aberdeen: A. King, 1896.

Pieper, Josef. *Leisure: the Basis of Culture,* trans. Alexander Dru. New York: Pantheon Books, 1964.

Plato. *Republic*: Book VII trans. Paul Shorey. New Jersey: Princeton University Press, 1980.

Rupert, Jane. *John Henry Newman on the Nature of the Mind: Reason in Religion, Science, the Humanities.* New York: Lexington Books, 2011.

Sayers, Dorothy. "Lost Tools of Learning," essay (1947). Accessed November 10, 2014. www.gbt.org/text/sayers.html

Schall, James V. *A Student's Guide to Liberal Learning.* Delaware: ISI Books, 2000.

Sheed, Frank. *Knowing God.* San Francisco: Ignatius Press, 2012.

Shrimpton, Paul. *A Catholic Eton? Newman's Oratory School.* Leominster, UK:Gracewing, 2005.

Spitzer, Robert. *New Proofs for the Existence of God.* Grand Rapids: W.B. Eerdmans Publishing Co, 2010.

St. John Paul II. *Ex Corde Ecclesiae* [Apostolic Constitution on Catholic Universities]. Accessed November 10, 2014. http://www.vatican.va/holy_father/john_paul_ii/apost_consti tutions/documents/hf_jp-ii_apc_15081990_ex-corde-ecclesiae_en.html.

St. Augustine of Hippo. *The Confessions*, trans. Maria Goulding, O.S.B. San Francisco: Ignatius Press, 2012.

Thomas Aquinas. *Summa Theologiae,* I-II, Q27, Article 1

Tolkien, J.R. *The Letters of J.R. Tolkien*, ed Humphrey Carpenter and Christopher Tolkien. Boston: Houghton Mifflin, 1981.

Vélez, Juan R. *Passion for Truth, The Life of John Henry Newman.* Charlotte: TAN Books, 2012.

Virgil. *Aeneid,* trans John Dryden. New York: P F Collier & Son, 1909. Accessed November 10, 2014. http://www.perseus.tufts.edu/hopper/text?doc=Perseus%3 Atext%3A1999.02.0052%3Abook%3D1%3Acard%3D1

Virgil. *The Aeneid of Virgil,* trans. by Robert Fagles. New York: Viking Books, 2006.

Voegelin, Eric. *Order and History, Vol. III: Plato and Aristotle.* Louisiana: Louisiana State University Press, 1957.

Wilhelmsen, Frederick D. "The Great Books, Enemies of Wisdom,"
    Modern Age. 30 (1987): 323-331. Accessed November 10,
    2014. www.mmisi.org/ma/31_3-4/wilhemsen.pdf

Woods, Thomas E., *How the Catholic Church Built Western
    Civilization.* Washington: Regnery History, 2005.

Alighiere, Dante, *Divine Comedy*, 87, 91, 93

Adams, John, 23-24, 78

Adler, Mortimer, J., 94

Alma Mater, 39, 52, 62, 123-124

Applied Sciences, 19, 22, 9 96-97, 107

Aquinas, St. Thomas, Ipsum Esse Subsistens, 20, 70, 73, 90, 94, 144, 147, 161
Beauty, definition, 137

Architecture, 80, 110, 123, 134, 151

Aristotle, 20, 25-26, 29, 32, 49, 73, 84-85, 90-91, 98-99, 105, 124, 126, 135, 141

Art, 7, 28-29, 40, 47-48, 71, 76, 80, 84, 88, 93, 100, 131, 135, 137, 139, 149, 152, 156

Augustine of Hippo, St., 70, 73, 79, 88-90, 104, 110, 120, 144; *The Confessions*, 79, 88; *The City of God*, 89, 110

Beauty, 15, 25, 47-48, 50, 65, 82, 88-89, 134, 137

Benedictine Order, 159

Benedict XVI, 35, 81, 133, 145, 164; Enc. *Spe salvi*, 100

Biology, 41, 64, 71, 73, 92, 97-98, 101, 131, 133

Bloom, Allan, *The Closing of the American Mind*, 15-16, 38, 40-42, 44, 48, 51, 129, 141

Boethius, Anicius Manlius Severinus, 70, 89, 141

Buckley, William, *God and Man at Yale*, 63-64, 79, 81

Catholic Student Centers, 112, 116, 124

Catholic University of Ireland, 11, 19, 26, 121-122, 125-126, 145, 163

Catholicism, Anti-Catholic prejudice, 65-66, 110, 165

Cervantes, Miguel de, 23, 93

Charlemagne, 155, 158, 161; Charlemagne's Schools, 154

Choosing the Right College, selection criteria, 52, 62, 147

Cicero, Marcus Tullius, 23, 28, 32, 46, 85, 87-90, 93, 164

Classical Greek Literature, 82

College, 9, 15-18, 21-23, 33, 35-36, 39, 41-46, 52-53, 55-62, 68-69, 77-78, 96, 112-115, 117-122, 124, 126-130, 133-134, 137-138, 140, 142-144, 147-149, 156, 159-161, 165; definition, 15; selection criteria, 55-57; cost, 58-59

Colleges and Halls, 57, 77, 121, 124, 146, 148, 159-161

Colleges and Universities, 13, 16, 18, 22-23, 29, 38, 41, 45-46, 49, 59, 63-65, 76, 92, 107, 110, 112, 118, 124, 129, 135, 142-143, 161-163; Beaumont College, 159; Benedictine College, 112; Boston College, 65; Bowdoin College, 42; Christendom College, 39; Columbia University, 40,94; Franciscan University, 39; Georgetown University, 65; Harvard University, 23, 42, 64, 134; Humboldt University of Berlin, 40; Johns Hopkins University, 40; Maynooth College, 161; OxfordUniversity, 2, 19; Princeton University, 9, 64;

Simon Bolivar University, 108; St. John's College, 40

Thomas Aquinas College, 39-40; University of Chicago, 40-41, 94, 120; University of Dallas, 39; University of Illinois, 112; University of Kansas, 11, 71, 120; University of Navarre, 8, 39, 118, 141, 176; University of Notre Dame, 40, 65; Yale University 63, 81

College graduates, 127, 129-130, 134, 144, 147

College students, 10, 45, 55-56, 57, 77, 130, 176

Conley, James D., Most Reverend, 7, 11, 144

Constantine, Emperor, 81

Core Curriculum, classical Core curriculum, 22, 39, 46-48, 51, 53, 144,

Council of Trent, 154-155, 161

Culture, 17, 20, 22, 32-33, 41, 44, 47, 49, 64-65, 80-82, 85, 110-111, 115, 127-128, 135-139, 142-143, 145, 148, 152, 154, 166; definition, 80 Christian culture, 81-82; And religion, 139-140; Greek and Roman culture, 80, 82, 85,

91, 151; Western culture, 30, 32, 43, 45, 80, 88, 92, 94, 138, 142-143; (see also American Culture, 40)

Darwin, Charles, 104

Dentistry, 126-127, 131

Einstein, Albert, 67, 105-106

Engineering, 9-10, 15, 18, 20, 31, 41, 69, 96-97, 126, 133-134, 151

Escrivá, St. Josemaría, 39, 141, 145

Finances, financial aid, 52, 58-59, 148

Fine Arts, 47-48, 53, 137, 143, 151

Friendship, A Community of Friends, 11, 21, 26, 49-50, 52, 112, 120-121, 124, 139, 146

Future Generations, 129, 137-138, 143

Galilei, Galileo, 64, 68, 100, 104

Gentleman, 8, 33-34, 83, 117, 139; definition, 34

God, existence, 72-73, 79, 109; God and man, 77; *God*

and Man at Yale, 63, 79, 81 God in the classrooms, 63, 67, 77

Government, career, 127

Graduate Studies, history, 108, 128-129, 132, 134

Higher Education, opening of the mind, 9-10, 13, 15-16, 18, 20-23, 35-36, 38, 42-43, 45-46, 51-54, 57, 59-60, 62, 64-65, 77, 110-111, 141, 144; The purpose, 23, 35; (see also higher learning, 15, 39, 65, 143, 163)

Holy Bible, 29, 47, 76-77, 88, 91, 93, 112, 148; composition, 76; translations, 91 (see also Sacred Scriptures, 28, 70, 76-77, 89, 93, 104, 112, 135, 152); (see also Holy Scriptures, 63, 79, 88)

Homer, *Iliad*, *Odyssey*, 48, 82-83, 85-86, 93-95, 143-144

Humanities, 8, 11-12, 22, 29-31, 41, 107-108, 126, 128-129, 133-135, 137, 147, 158

Idea of a University, 11-12, 19, 24, 26, 34, 50, 83, 95-96, 102-103, 123, 128, 146

Intellect, 9, 11, 18, 26, 29, 31,

171

33-35, 52, 68, 106, 127,
142, 145-146; cultivation,
22, 25, 38, 111, 139

John Paul II, St., 65, 68,
112, 144-145; Enc. *Fides et
Ratio*, 68; Apost. Exhortation
Ex Corde Ecclesiae, 65

Knowledge, 11, 13, 18-20,
22, 25-27, 30-31, 33-35,
38, 41-42, 49-50, 55,
68-71, 74-75, 77-78, 82,
92-93, 96-97, 99-108,
116-117, 122-123, 126,
128, 130-131, 133, 135,
139, 142, 144-146, 151,
156, 163; Highest, 20;
Ordering of the sciences,
69-73; Pursuit of, 20, 32, 119;
Skepticism, 16, 20, 68, 120;
Truth, 35, 107; Universal, 162;
Whole of, 42, 50;
Dominus Illuminatio Mea, 2

Law (Degree), 18, 23,
150-151, 156

Law Career, 23, 126;
St. Thomas More, 91, 133;
St. Alphonsus Ligouri, 132

Languages, 28, 53, 55, 87,
89, 92, 94, 130, 156, 162

Languages and Literature,
80, 136-137

Latin, language, 23, 28-29,

32-33, 46, 80, 85-88, 90-94,
105, 150; Liturgy, 93-94

Learning, 7-9, 15, 18-19,
22, 25-28, 30-39, 41-42, 50,
52-54, 61, 65, 73, 84, 92, 97,
100, 108, 116, 119, 123, 126,
135, 143-144, 151-158,
161, 163; for Learning's
Sake, 30, 158

Leisure, 32-33

Liberal Arts, 17, 21-23, 34,
36, 38, 41, 43, 45, 50, 52-53,
56, 90, 98, 107-108, 110, 120,
126, 128, 131-132, 134-135,
137-138, 140, 142, 144;
Liberal Arts Colleges, 41-42,
45, 53, 78; Liberal Arts
Degree (Courses), 107-108,
126-128, 137, 140, 147;
Liberal Arts Education, 16, 20
22-23, 38, 43, 45, 48-49, 52,
96-97, 127-128, 120, 131-133,
131-133, 139-140, 144-145

Lejeune, Jérôme, 108-109

Lemaître, Georges, Big Bang
Theory, 66, 106

Literature, 11-12, 28-31, 40,
43, 47, 49, 53, 63-64, 66, 71,
76-77, 80, 82, 85, 87, 89, 91-93,
126, 135-138, 143-144, 157,
161-162; 20th century
authors, 144-145

Longo, Bl. Bartolo, 132

Mansfield, Harvey, 42, 43-44

McInerny, Ralph, 46, 50, 94

Medicine, 16, 18, 23, 41, 69, 96, 105, 118, 126-127, 131, 149-150, 156-157

Monks, Irish, English, 11, 80, 89, 90, 152-155, 157, 159-160

Morality, 50, 57-58, 62, 74-75, 107, 115, 132, 139

Music, 7, 28, 31, 47-48, 52, 55, 80, 121, 137-139, 149, 155

Natural Sciences, 20-21, 25, 41, 96-101, 105, 107, 129, 133, 135, 147, 149, 163; History, 98

Natural Theology, 70, 72-75, 112, 120, 143; definition, 70

Newman Centers, 13, 61 116, 122

Newman, John Henry, Education, 8-9, 11-13, 15, 19, 20, 24, 26-28, 31-32, 34-35, 39, 50, 54, 57, 61, 74-75, 78, 82-83, 85, 87-88, 90, 95-96, 102, 109, 125-128, 136, 138-139, 146, 149-150, 153-154, 156-158, 160, 162-163; Establishment of the Catholic University of Ireland, 11, 19, 121, 126, 145, 162-163; Oratory School, 88, 124; Oriel College, 26, 78, 121-122; Trinity College, 78, 121; *Rise and Progress of Universities*, 19, 149, 162
See *Idea of a University*

Nursing, 15, 131

Personal Objectives, 54

Pharmacy, 96, 131

Philosophy, 9-10, 12-13, 20, 26, 28-30, 34, 40, 42, 46-47, 53, 63, 69-71, 73-74, 79, 83-85, 87, 89, 94, 97, 99, 103, 107, 118, 126, 130, 132, 135, 137-138, 140-141, 143, 147, 149-152, 155, 157-158

Philosophical Habit of Mind, 21, 45, 108, 126, 142

Pieper, Josef, 32-33, 145,

Plato, 16, 20, 25-26, 49, 70, 84, 132, 135, 140-141
His works, Parable of the Cave, *The Republic*, 25, 84, 140-141

Pope Gregory, 151

Portillo, Bl. Alvaro del, 39

Prayer, 61-62, 89, 94,
112-114, 116, 121, 139, 143;
and university life, 33,
110-111

Professional Schools, 18, 22,
28, 36, 38-39, 128-129, 131

Professors, choice of, 20, 49

Quadrivium, 28, 90, 150,
155, 159

Religious Freedom, see
Religious liberty, 57, 111

Roman Literature and
Culture, 85

Science, 10, 12, 16, 18, 20,
22, 26, 30-31, 34, 38, 40-42,
46-47, 60, 63, 67, 71, 73, 83,
92, 96-97, 99-109, 118-119,
126-128, 131-135, 138-139,
142, 144, 151, 155-156, 162;
Foundations and Limits
of Science, 101; Harmony
Between Science and
Faith, 103, 109, 133,
143, Scientific method,
99, 101-102, 107,119

Scientists, 9, 21, 40,
98, 100-105, 107-109,
139-140, 143, 149;
Aristotle, 20, 25-26, 28-29,

32, 49, 73, 84-85, 90-91,
98-99, 105, 124, 135, 141;
Francis Bacon, 100;
Claudius Galen of Pergamon,
99, 150; Galileo, 68, 100,
104; Isaac Newton, 100;
Carl Sagan, 103, 105; Albert
the Great, 20, 105, 161; Gregor
Mendel
105; Louis Pasteur, 105;
Albert Einstein, 67, 105-106;
Shinya Yamanaka, 140

Sexuality, 43, 78, 115, 148

Shakespeare, William,
47-48, 52

Shrimpton, Paul, 19, 122,
124, 126, 146, 149, 163; *A
Catholic Eton? Newman's
Oratory School*, 124

Spiritual Life of Christian
Students, 111-112

Social Sciences, 41, 126, 129,
132, 135, 147

Socrates, 25-26, 49, 84, 135,
140

The Classics and Western
Culture, 80

The Fellowship of Catholic
University Students (FOCUS),
112

Theology, 11, 16, 26, 30, 53, 63, 66-76, 78, 88, 94, 96, 100-101, 103-105, 107, 126, 132- 133, 135, 138, 143, 147, 156-157; definition, 68; Study of in the Medieval University, 69, 135

The Soul, 13, 15-18, 23, 25, 27, 31, 38, 49, 51, 63-64, 71, 73, 96, 102, 110, 114, 131, 140-141, 144, 146; Its perfections, 31; Opening of the mind, 143; Enlargement of/Magnanimity, 31, 49

Trivium, 28, 90, 150, 155, 159

Tutor, mentors, 8, 22-23, 36, 50, 121-124, 130, 160

Universities, 8-9, 12-13, 16, 20, 22, 28-31, 34-36, 39-41, 53, 61, 63, 65-66, 69, 71-72,76, 79, 90, 96, 107-108, 110-111, 116, 118, 120-121, 130-135, 144, 149, 154-156, 158-163, Origins, 20, 134-135, 149; First Universities, 156-158; Athens, 20, 28, 83-84, 90, 149, 155; Alexandria, 90, 149-150,152, 155; German, 40, 158; Medieval universities, 28, 69, 90, 135,

149, 155-156,163; Roman Empire, 85-86, 93, 150-151, 154; United States, 13, 15-16, 23, 30, 39, 40-42, 45, 47, 63, 65, 76, 81, 92, 94, 111-113, 126

University Education, 8-9, 10, 13, 17-22, 25, 31,33, 39, 45, 47, 50, 53, 71, 82, 91, 94, 107, 110, 122, 133, 142-143 The purpose, 17, 22

University study, end of university studies, 17, 18, 23, 33, 124, 126, 129, 140

Useful Education, Lord Brougham, Lord Shaftesbury, 31, 34-35, (see also useful knowledge, 34, 116, 142, 151)

Virgil, 23, 46, 85, 86-87, 90-91, 93, 95; *The Aeneid*, 87, 91, 95

Virtue, 16, 18, 25-26, 31, 33, 35, 38, 51, 70, 82, 86, 99, 110-111, 116-117, 121, 123-124, 132, 138-139,

Western Civilization, 39, 41, 50, 68, 76, 79, 104, 136, 149

Will, Christian morality, 8, 9, 23, 25-27, 33, 38, 45, 52-53 60, 97, 112, 132

Wisdom, 13, 19-20, 22, 26-27, 29, 37, 44-45, 49-50, 69-70, 72, 75-76, 79, 89, 97, 108, 117, 136, 140, 143

Laus Deo Virginique Matri

ABOUT THE AUTHOR

Fr. Vélez was born in Venezuela and grew up in Colombia and the United States. He has also lived in England, Spain and Italy. His earlier professional formation was as a physician specialized in internal medicine. In 1998, he obtained a doctorate in Dogmatic Theology at the University of Navarre with a thesis on Cardinal Newman's teaching on life after death. The same year he was ordained a priest of the Prelature of Opus Dei and since then has served as a priest in various cities of the United States, often providing human and spiritual formation to college students.

Made in the USA
San Bernardino, CA
26 April 2015